Steve Jones

I pray that God uses all
7 Keys to the
your life an
life!
Becky —

7
KEYS
TO
THE
ANOINTING

"We have this treasure in earthen vessels"

Becky Farina Cain

7 *Keys To The Anointing*
"We have this treasure in earthen vessels"
by Becky Farina Cain

Printed in the United States of America

ISBN 9781615795543

www.xulonpress.com

CONTENTS

ACKNOWLEDGEMENTS

I want to thank God the Father, God the Son, and God the Holy Spirit for allowing me to write this book. Without Your Presence and Anointing, life would not even be worth living! I love You with all my heart, mind, soul and strength!

I want to thank my very best friend, and my high school sweetheart, Eddie, my adorable husband of thirty-two years! Eddie has stood by me and given me his one hundred percent support for which I will always be grateful! I couldn't have done it without you! I love you, Baby, and I will love you forever!

Thank you to my children, their spouses and my precious grandson: Jennifer, Trey, Eric, Liz and Peyton! I love you with all of my heart and will eternally love you no matter what! I am proud of all of you as I watch you grow more in love with Jesus!

Special thanks to my parents Ted and Geneva Farina who are looking down from heaven at me today! Without such a loving and godly home environment, I wouldn't be the woman of God that I am today. Thank you for your support and encouragement that I could be anything God wanted me to be!

Thank you to my siblings and their families—Terri, Paul, Tim, Beth, Teddy and Kristi! You all have been there when I have been in need! You have supported me one hundred percent. I love each and every one of you. Thanks for helping with the editing, Tim. Tim, I am typing this book on the laptop you "loaned" me! Thanks!

Thank you, Mary Ledford, for all of your hard work in editing and for the encouragement you have given me! I cannot thank you enough! Thank you, Keith Ledford, for letting your sweetheart of 48 years spend time on this book when she could have spent the time with you! I love you both dearly!

INTRODUCTION

2 Corinthians 4:7 AMP
7 However, we possess this precious treasure [the
divine Light of the Gospel] in [frail, human] vessels
of earth that the grandeur and exceeding greatness
of the power may be shown to be from God and not
from ourselves.

I was sitting in my bedroom in Florida on February 10, 2007 at 3:20 a.m., watching International House of Prayer on *God TV*. As Mike Bickle began to prophesy, I had a vision. I saw an old-fashioned fountain pen with a gold tip. I heard, "Write as a scribe." I saw a book title, but it was a bit blurry. I saw a gold key holder with golden keys. The cover of the book was an amber, golden cover. I heard the name "7 Keys to the Anointing". Then, I heard God tell me that He was mandating me to write the book "7 Keys to the Anointing". I heard write the above information down. After that, I saw a burlap scrap under an aged bronze treasure chest and heard the scripture (2 Corinthians 4:7) "We have this treasure in earthen vessels".

Over the years I have had many prophecies that I would be a writer of books and that I was to be like a "prophetic scribe". Until I received this vision and word from God on February 10, 2007, I chose not to just "write a book". To the best of my ability, I have tried to write only what the Holy Spirit dictated to me—to be a "prophetic scribe".

As you read this book, I know that the Holy Spirit will bring to life those areas He wrote through me for you. I pray that you not only allow the Anointing to come to you to touch you, or to come into you to change you, but flow through you to touch and change the world!

CHAPTER ONE

A DOOR IS NOT CLOSED TO YOU WHEN YOU HOLD THE KEY TO OPEN IT!

Luke 11:52 AMP
52 Woe to you, lawyers (experts in the Mosaic
Law)! For you have taken away the key to
knowledge; you did not go in yourselves, and you
hindered and prevented those who were entering

Matthew 16:19 AMP
19 I will give you the keys of the kingdom of heaven;
and whatever you bind (declare to be improper and
unlawful) on earth must be what is already bound in
heaven; and whatever you loose (declare lawful) on
earth must be what is already loosed in heaven.

Have you ever locked your keys in your car? Have you ever locked yourself out of your home? For some of you, this may bring back some infuriating memories, for others some hilarious memories.

I was always glad to know that my dad, Ted Farina, was on the right side of the law! Whenever anyone would lock their keys in their car, my dad had a special knack of taking a wire hanger and twisting it just so to unlock the car door so the keys could be retrieved. Of course, that was back in the day before the new, improved gadgets to lock and unlock car doors. My dad was known to take a credit card and unlock the door of our house to get us in when the keys had been left inside. However, the best way to open a door is with the keys!

Speaking of keys, I received the following email:

A cop saw a woman down on her knees under a streetlight.
"Can I help you?" he asked
Replied the woman, "I dropped my keys and
I'm looking for them."
"Are you sure you dropped them right here?"
"No." responded the blonde, "I dropped them down in that
alley, but it's way too dark to find anything down there."

Now as funny as that email is, we too, need to make sure we are looking in the right place for our God-given keys. You are not going to find the keys to the Anointing anywhere but at the feet of Jesus. At least the woman got the right posture—she was down on her knees!

Since the title of this book is "7 Keys to the Anointing", the first thing we are going to do is to take a look into the Bible definition of the word "key". What is a key? According to <u>Nelson's Illustrated Bible Dictionary</u> a key is:

> ➤ The tool that releases a lock (Judges 3:25).
> ➤ The key is also spoken of symbolically in the Bible as a sign of authority. The prophet Isaiah described a time when Eliakim, son of Hilkiah, would be elevated as the king's steward (2 Kings 18:18). The

prophet declared that He would be given "the key of the House of David" (Isaiah 22:22), or the authority to act in the king's name. This is probably the background for a proper understanding of the statement of Jesus that the "keys of the kingdom of heaven" were being given to Peter (Matthew 16:19). As the Messiah from the line of David, Jesus was calling on Peter to take on leadership responsibility for the young church.

➤ Jesus condemned the SCRIBES of His day because they had "taken away the key of knowledge" (Luke 11:52). According to their interpretation, only they had the right to explain the meaning of God's Law, or the Scriptures. They failed to share this knowledge with the common people. [1]

According to www.yourdictionary.com some of the definitions for the word "key" are:

1) An instrument, usually of metal for moving the bolt of a lock and thus locking or unlocking something

2) Any of several instruments or mechanical devices resembling or suggesting this in form or use; specif.,

    a) A device to turn a bolt, etc. *a skate key, a watch key*

    b) A pin, bolt, wedge, cotter, or similar device put into a hole or space to lock or hold parts together

    c) *A device for opening and closing an electric circuit [Italics mine]*

    d) A key-shaped emblem presented as an honor *the key to the city*

3) Something regarded as like a key in opening a way, revealing or concealing, etc.; specif.,

a) A place so located as to give access to or control of a region *Vicksburg was the key to the lower Mississippi*

b) A thing that explains or solves something else, as a book of answers, the explanations on a map, the code to a system of pronunciation, etc.

c) A controlling or essential person or thing

A key can represent authority given. We as believers have been given the "keys of the kingdom of heaven"—authority keys, spoken of in Matthew 16:19. As you read this book, you are going to receive the "7 Keys to the Anointing". Just as you have to choose to apply the "keys of the kingdom of heaven" in order for them to work, you must also choose to apply the 7 Keys that are going to unlock the Anointing in your life. A key is not useful to you if you leave it sitting in a drawer.

We are going to explore "7 Keys to the Anointing", keys that will unlock the correct doors of the Anointing. A door may look like it is closed to you, but if you have the right key and you position the key into the lock and disengage the lock, the door suddenly becomes an "open door". It is a good thing to keep in mind *that a door is not closed to you when you hold the key to open it!*

CHAPTER TWO

WHAT IS THE ANOINTING?

We must discover what the Anointing is. Thank God for the Anointing! The Anointing is a tangible substance. The Anointing is God's ability, efficiency and might that come upon an individual to serve the Body of Christ. I heard Kenneth E. Hagin, Sr. say on Television "The Anointing is a heavenly materiality! The Anointing is perceptible to the touch. The Anointing is capable of being touched." The bottom line is "The Anointing" is God's manifested Presence and power. It is greater than all the power of the devil.

"Manifested Presence" verses "Omnipresence"

Since "the Anointing" is God's "Manifested Presence", we should not confuse God's "Manifested Presence" with the fact that God is "Omnipresent". To be omnipresent is the ability to be everywhere at all times and God is present everywhere at all times. The Bible tells us in Matthew 6:4 that God Who sees in secret will reward you openly. Even though God is everywhere at all times, there are those times when God chooses to manifest or give visible, apparent evidence of His Presence at a certain place and time. That is what the Anointing is.

When God anoints you, when His manifested Presence touches you, you hold a sacred trust to be faithful to the undeserved free gift of the Holy Spirit and His Anointing He lavishes upon you. The Anointing is not to be taken lightly; it is a sacred trust to be cherished and cultivated. The Anointing is not to be exploited for your own personal gain. We must allow the Anointing to come upon us and touch us. Then we must also allow the Anointing to come in us to change us and then ultimately allow the Anointing to flow through us to touch and change our world! Let us remain faithful to the One whose name is "Faithful"!

Levels of the Anointing

There are levels of the Anointing. The level we walk in depends on how hungry we are for God's Presence. We must be aware that since the Anointing is the tangible, manifested Presence of God, we can allow the Anointing or God's tangible, manifested Presence:

To flow to us to touch us.
To flow in us to change us.
To flow through us to touch and change our world!

Too many people only want to allow the Anointing to "flow to them to touch them". You can easily spot them. They come to a Holy Spirit anointed service. They get in line for prayer. They may fall in the Spirit and may laugh, shake and such, but they never change. They have what I call a "Party Spirit". They just want to "feel" something—to get some kind of thrill. They do not want to allow the Holy Spirit to change them. A touch is not enough! As Ecclesiastes 3:1 tells us, "there is a time for everything". I add—a time to sit, soak and get anointed with the Presence and power of the Holy Spirit and a time to take what you've received and get up and go tell, heal, deliver, set free and be obedient! We must allow God to change us into the image of Christ Jesus [see Romans 8:29]!

Ezekiel 47:1-7, 12 AMP
1 THEN HE [my guide] brought me again to the
door of the house [of the Lord—the temple], and
behold, waters issued out from under the threshold
of the temple toward the east, for the front of the
temple was toward the east; and the waters came
down from under, from the right side of the temple,
on the south side of the altar.
2 Then he brought me out by way of the north gate
and led me around outside to the outer gate by
the way that faces east, and behold, waters were
running out on the right side. [Zechariah 14:8;
Revelation 22:1,2.]
3 And when the man went on eastward with the
measuring line in his hand, he measured a thousand
cubits, and he caused me to pass through the
waters, waters that were ankle-deep.4 Again he
measured a thousand cubits and caused me to pass
through the waters, waters that reached to the
knees. Again he measured a thousand cubits and
caused me to pass through the waters,
waters that reached to the loins.
5 Afterward he measured a thousand, and it was a
river that I could not pass through, for the waters
had risen, waters to swim in, a river that could not
be passed over or through.
6 And he said to me, Son of man, have you seen
this? Then he led me and caused me to return to the
bank of the river.
7 Now when I had returned, behold, on the bank of
the river were very many trees on the

one side and on the other.
12 And on the banks of the river on both its sides,
there shall grow all kinds of trees for food; their leaf
shall not fade nor shall their fruit fail [to meet the
demand]. Each tree shall bring forth new fruit every
month, [these supernatural qualities being] because
their waters came from out of the sanctuary. And
their fruit shall be for food and
their leaves for healing.

Revelation 22:1-2 AMP
1 THEN HE showed me the river whose waters
give life, sparkling like crystal, flowing out from the
throne of God and of the Lamb
2 Through the middle of the broadway of the city;
also, on either side of the river was the tree of life
with its Twelve varieties of fruit, yielding each
month its fresh crop; and the leaves of the tree were
for the healing and the restoration of the nations.

The manifested Presence of God or the Anointing is also revealed in The River of God. There is no doubt that the River in Ezekiel is the same river referred to in the book of Revelation! The book of Revelation gets even more specific concerning where the river's starting place is. Not only does the river flow from the temple as stated in Ezekiel 47:1, but it begins from the throne of God and of the Lamb, Jesus Christ! Revelation 22:2 and Ezekiel 47:12 both state there are trees on both sides of the river which will bring forth fruit every month and the leaves will be for healing! More importantly, did you know that the same River of God could flow from you? Why? Because, according to I Corinthians 3:16-17, if you have received Jesus Christ as your Lord and Savior then you yourself are God's temple and God's Spirit lives in you.

It is up to you whether you are ankle deep or swimming in the Presence of God!

As I was teaching on this passage one Sunday evening, I had a vision of "The River of God" coming from the throne of God and through my back, then through my stomach and then out to everyone around me. The Bible calls the stomach our innermost being or belly [John 7:38] depending on the translation of the Bible. Our goal should be to let God's River or His Anointing not only flow to us, but also change us and flow through us to change others!

When we misuse the Anointing of the Holy Spirit by being only a receiver and not a giver, we become like the Dead Sea. The Dead Sea receives water from the Jordan River and four or five other streams, but it does not have an outlet. Its waters are said to be bitter and it stinks. The water is nauseating to the taste. Its buoyancy is so great that it is difficult to sink the limbs deep enough for swimming in contrast to the River of God spoken of in Ezekiel 47:5, where the waters are to swim in.[1] In order to be spiritually healthy and keep a continuous flow of the Anointing of the Holy Spirit, we must not only receive, but we must give out—otherwise, we will become bitter, nauseating and stinky to those around us and to God.

Ezekiel 47:9 AMP
9 And wherever the double river shall go, every living creature which swarms shall live. And there shall be a very great number of fish, because these waters go there that [the waters of the sea] may be healed and made fresh; and everything shall live wherever the river goes

When you, as God's CARRIER of His anointed River, go out [allowing God's River to flow through you to touch and change the world], there will be a great number of fish, which represents many salvations. Many people will also be healed spiritually, physically, mentally and financially, as you allow the River of God to flow through you. Remember God is the Source. We are not The Source. God, "The Source", is flowing to you and through you! As Zechariah 4:6 says in the Amplified version, *"It's not by might, nor by power, but by My Spirit [of Whom the oil is a symbol] says the Lord of hosts."* We just have to YIELD to the Holy Spirit and let Him do the work through us!

Never the Same Again

If you allow the Holy Spirit to not only come upon you to touch you, but to come in you to change you, you will find yourself not being able to watch certain television programs or participate in certain conversations. This is not a legalistic thing, but the closer you get to God the more sensitive you become to the things that offend Him. I remember being in the kitchen making dinner and the television was on in the family room when all of the sudden a curse word was spoken on the program. It offended me. I had to turn the program off. I must add that you must maintain a close relationship with the Holy Spirit because we leak! You can tell when you begin to leak. What once bothered you because you were so sensitive to the Holy Spirit, no longer bothers you. This is not a one-time experience. It is a lifetime pursuit!

The Anointing Makes All The Difference!

Have you ever heard two or three different people sing the same song, but one of them just seemed to touch your heart like the other two were not able to do? Then to add a little more confusion, the person whose singing touched your heart was not quite as talented as one of the other people. What do you think was different about the one that moved you? Obviously it was not the song. They all sang the same song. The difference was "the Anointing"! It's as if heaven comes down to earth and kisses the song through the singer. When a singer allows the Holy Spirit to anoint his/her singing, the result is that it brings glory to God and moves people.

What about a song that no matter who sings it, it moves your heart? There are songs that for some reason it doesn't matter who sings them they touch your heart. The answer is that there are songs that are anointed by the Holy Spirit. These songs become what we call "classics". One of my favorite "classic" hymns that falls into the category of "anointed songs" is "How Great Thou Art"!

My sister-in-law, Beth, who used to play in our church band in the 1990's, is an anointed flautist. She would know by the Holy Spirit when to begin to play her flute at just the right moments, with just the right sounds. It would move the praise and worship up another notch! In Beth's case, she was extremely talented as well as anointed!

When an anointed song is combined with anointed musicians, God's Presence is accelerated to an even higher level! During the time my husband and I were Evangelists, we would frequently get comments from people that they were literally physically healed while we were singing a certain song. Others commented that they were set free as we were singing. The Anointing makes all the difference! Elizabeth Moore of Clinton Maryland who received a spiritual healing as we sang an anointed song says:

I would like to share a brief testimony with you about a spiritual healing. My walk with God was growing cold and prayer was boring and reading my Bible was a duty. I was finding nothing exciting about God or His Word. As a matter of fact, I was beginning to wonder if God was doing or could do anything

*these days. I was beginning to grow angry and nega-
tive, because I knew where I should be and yet was
not. I could only feel coldness creeping in, and I was
getting scared. Then He [God] sent the two of you
[Eddie and Becky Cain], and WOW!!! The first night
you were here you sang a song about the woman
with the issue of blood and there is a verse in there
that says "and suddenly a touch from heaven, Jesus
came and rescued me"…etc. That is what He did for
me. I felt the power of the Holy Spirit touch me that
night and I shook like a leaf on a tree and I began to
weep and some how I knew, that I knew, that I knew
that God was and is and is still God and that He still
moves and reigns. He rekindled the fire in me and
I have decided that what God has I want and I'm
going for it. I thank you for allowing the Holy Spirit
to minister through you. You create an atmosphere
for Him to move. It's very humbling to lay prostrate
on the floor before God and allow Him to deal with
you, but I would not pass up the chance for the world.
I have regained the excitement and joy I had before
and I have such a hunger for God. It's exciting and I
can't wait to see what He does next.*

The Anointing on a song sets people free. The Anointing
can even give you favor in your work place so that you get
promoted before more educated people or before those who
have greater tenure than you do. I am not against education,
but education alone is not the answer. Allow the Holy Spirit
to place His Anointing upon every area of your life and
watch what happens!

Destroys

Isaiah 10:27 KJV
27 And it shall come to pass in that day, that his
burden shall be taken away from off thy shoulder,
and his yoke from off thy neck, and the yoke shall be
destroyed because of the anointing.

Isaiah 10:27 tells us that the Anointing destroys the yoke. You can drop a glass coffee cup on a tile floor and it will probably get broken. Yet, there is a possibility that the coffee cup can be glued together again. However, when something is destroyed it cannot be repaired again. Praise God, when the Anointing comes it will completely destroy any and every yoke of bondage in our lives!

When we allow the Holy Spirit Anointing to come upon us to touch and change us, then He uses us to touch and change the world. Touching heaven and changing earth! It is of utmost importance that we "become" whom God created us to be—men, women, boys and girls who walk in God's love. Many of the people who are touched and changed through our obedience will then in turn allow the Holy Spirit to anoint them to touch and change their world! It is the gift that keeps on giving.

CHAPTER THREE

OIL AND THE ANOINTING

Zechariah 4:6 AMP

*6 Then he said to me, This [addition of the bowl
to the candlestick, causing it to yield a ceaseless
supply of oil from the olive trees] is the word of
the Lord to Zerubbabel, saying, Not by might, nor
by power, but by My Spirit [of Whom the oil is a
symbol], says the Lord of hosts.*

We read in Zechariah 4:6 that oil is a symbol of the
Holy Spirit or of the Anointing. In the Old Testament
the most common word for "Anointing" is the Hebrew word
"mashach", which means, "to anoint by rubbing with oil as
a means of consecration; also to paint". [1] Anointing with oil,
therefore, was a symbol of endowment with the Spirit of God
for duties of the office to which a person was consecrated.
So we can say that oil can be a symbol of the Holy Spirit and
His empowerment.

The most common word for "Anointing" in the New
Testament is the Greek word "chrio" [Acts 10:38] which
translates to "to smear or rub with oil as a means of consecration to an office or religious service" [2] Oil being the
common denominator, today we usually see people anointed

with a dab of oil placed upon their foreheads. In some religious circles, the oil is drawn on the forehead in the sign of a cross. In the Old Testament, the oil would be poured over their heads, saturating their hair and flowing down onto their clothes [Psalms 133:2].

"The first instance of the religious use of oil is the Anointing of the stone by Jacob (Genesis 28:18; 35:14), evidently designed to be a formal consecration of the stone, or spot, to a sacred purpose. Under the Mosaic law persons and things set apart for sacred purposes were anointed with the "holy Anointing oil" [Exodus 30:23-25, 30-33]." [3]

Exodus 30:30-33 AMP
30 And you shall anoint Aaron and his sons and sanctify (separate) them, that they may minister to Me as priests.
31 And say to the Israelites, This is a holy anointing oil [symbol of the Holy Spirit], sacred to Me alone throughout your generations. [Romans 8:9; 1 Corinthians 12:3.]
32 It shall not be poured upon a layman's body, nor shall you make any other like it in composition; it is holy, and you shall hold it sacred.
33 Whoever compounds any like it or puts any of it upon an outsider shall be cut off from his people.

Exodus 30:32 makes it clear that the Anointing oil is so sacred that it is never to be used upon a layman's body. We should be very thankful that we are living under the New Covenant, which says that we are Kings and Priests unto our God [Revelation 1:5-6]! Therefore, God can anoint each and every one of us who call upon His Name! Praise God!

The word "anointed" in 1 John 2:20 means, "an ointment or smearing—the special endowment of the Holy Spirit—an unction." [4]

1 John 2:20 AMP
20 But you have been anointed] by [you hold a
sacred appointment from, you have been given an
unction from] the Holy one, and you all know [the
Truth] or you know all things.

As we can see in 1 John 2:20, it is the Holy Spirit Who anoints us. It is the Holy Spirit who will lead us into all the Truth. Take a moment to ask the Holy Spirit to give you "The Anointing of Truth" as you continue to read "The 7 Keys To The Anointing".

Should We Literally Anoint People With Oil?

Mark 6:12-13 AMP
12 So they went out and preached that men should
repent [that they should change their minds for
the better and heartily amend their ways, with
abhorrence of their past sins].
13 And they drove out many unclean spirits and
anointed with oil many who were
sick and cured them.

In Mark 6:13 the disciples anointed with oil many who were sick and cured them as Jesus had instructed them before sending them out two by two. The word "oil" in verse 13 of Mark chapter six is the Greek word *"elaion"*, which means "olive oil".[5] That is why most religious organizations anoint people with olive oil today.

Should we literally anoint people with oil? The disciples anointed sick people with anointed olive oil and the people were cured. James 5:14 tells us if anyone is sick, he should call for the spiritual guides, the church elders and the elders should anoint the sick one with oil "in the Lord's Name". Verse 15 continues to state, "The prayer offered in faith [after being anointed with oil "in the Lord's Name"] will "*sozo*" or make whole the sick person and if the sick person has committed sins, he/she will be forgiven." [6] The answer is, "Yes", we should literally anoint people with oil. Dan Lawrence from Ada, Oklahoma shares this testimony about the power of Anointing with oil:

> *On the morning of January 28, 1996, I woke up and couldn't raise my right arm. I was in constant pain. After Sunday service, I went home and took some Motrin. It did not help whatsoever. Eddie and Becky Cain were in their second week of Revival. I was working in the nursery that night. At 9pm I went down for prayer. Eddie asked me to raise my arms. I told him that I couldn't raise my right arm. He touched my right shoulder, and I immediately felt a burning sensation in my shoulder. He then asked Becky to get the oil. Becky and Eddie put oil on my shoulder. The burning got hotter and hotter. My right arm started slowly to move up until it was over my head. The power of God was all over me. My shoulder has not hurt since. Praise God! Thank God for Eddie and Becky Cain and their ministry!*

> *John 9:6-7 AMP*
> *6 When He had said this, He spat on the ground and made clay (mud) with His saliva, and He spread it [as ointment] on the man's eyes.*
> *7 And He said to him, Go, wash in the Pool of Siloam—which means Sent. So he went and washed, and came back seeing.*

Is the literal Anointing with oil the only way to see people healed and delivered? No. There are many other ways to heal people such as the laying on of hands, the speaking of a Word from God, or as Jesus once did, spitting in the dirt to make mud and then applying it on the blind person's eyes who was completely healed. I don't think that most people would like to be the recipient nor the giver of the latter Anointing!

"The Oil of Joy" or as the Amplified Version says, "The Oil of Exultant Joy and Gladness above and beyond your companions!" is spoken about in Hebrews 1:9. The word oil here being the Greek word "chrio", "to smear or rub with oil as a means of consecration to an office or religious service. [7] The Greek word for joy, *"agalliasis"*, means "Exceeding Joy"! [8] How many of you want some of that? I do! I have received the "Oil of Joy" without anyone placing oil on me. It is exceedingly wonderful and part of The Kingdom of God. Romans 14:17 confirms that the Kingdom of God is not a matter of getting the food and drink we like, but the Kingdom of God is righteousness [that state which makes a person acceptable to God] and [heart] peace and joy in the Holy Spirit!

Jesus told us in Matthew 6:33 to seek [aim at and strive after] first of all His Kingdom and His righteousness [His way of doing and being right], and then all these things taken together will be given you besides. We need to go after God and His Anointing!

The Ten Virgins

Matthew 25:1-13
1 THEN THE kingdom of heaven shall be likened to
ten virgins who took their lamps and
went to meet the bridegroom.
2 five of them were foolish (thoughtless, without
forethought) and five were wise
(sensible, intelligent, and prudent).
3 For when the foolish took their lamps, they did
not take any [extra] oil with them;

*4 But the wise took flasks of oil along with them
[also] with their lamps.
5 While the bridegroom lingered and was slow in
coming, they all began nodding their heads,
and they fell asleep.
6 But at midnight there was a shout, Behold, the
bridegroom! Go out to meet him!
7 Then all those virgins got up and
put their own lamps in order.
8 And the foolish said to the wise, Give us some of
your oil, for our lamps are going out.
9 But the wise replied, There will not be enough for
us and for you; go instead to the dealers
and buy for yourselves.
10 But while they were going away to buy, the
bridegroom came, and those who were prepared
went in with him to the marriage feast;
and the door was shut.
11 Later the other virgins also came and said, Lord,
Lord, open [the door] to us!
12 But He replied, I solemnly declare to you, I do
not know you [I am not acquainted with you].
13 Watch therefore [give strict attention and be
cautious and active], for you know neither the day
nor the hour when the Son of Man will come.*

You cannot judge a book by its cover. Looks can be deceiving! First of all, there were ten virgins. The Bible does not give any distinction between the ten virgins in verse one. The ten virgins took their lamps to go out to meet the Bridegroom. So if you or I looked at them, they would have looked the same. You and I can pretend to be something we are not—like looking faithful to God or moving in the Anointing—and we might fool many people. Thankfully, God looks on the heart!

God then makes a distinction between the ten virgins in verse three. He divides them into two categories five wise and five foolish. The foolish virgins are considered foolish because they did not take any extra oil for their lamps with them. Remember, oil is one of the representations or symbols of the Anointing. The oil also represents the fuel that keeps the fire of love burning for Jesus, The Bridegroom. So we could say that the foolish virgins did not take any extra Anointing with them. The wise virgins took flasks of oil [the Anointing] along with their lamps.

This Is A Test

Galatians 6:9 AMP
9 And let us not lose heart and grow weary and faint in acting nobly and doing right, for in due time and at the appointed season we shall reap, if we do not loosen and relax our courage and faint.

Galatians 5:22-23 KJV
22 But the fruit of the Spirit is love, joy, peace, longsuffering, gentleness, goodness, faith,
23 Meekness, temperance: against such there is no law.

This is a true and funny story. During the three years Eddie and I were evangelizing, we held a revival in a church where one of the members was literally a bit on the mentally slow side. The pastor warned us ahead of time because at any given moment, she might yell out whatever was on her mind to her husband. Occasionally, she would use unbecoming language. Everyone loved her and understood her condition. One evening her husband, Vern, decided to come up for prayer, when all of the sudden this woman yelled out, "Don't go up there Vern, they'll make you faint!" Of course, with all the joy going around, the laughter fit right in. Vern came up anyway, went out in the Spirit and had a glorious time in the Lord.

The Bible tells us that we will reap if we do not faint. It was taking a long time for the Bridegroom to come. Galatians 5:22 lets us know that one of the fruits of the Spirit is long-suffering. This is our testing ground. What has God spoken to you that you are still waiting to see manifested? Don't quit! Don't give up! I cannot tell you how many times Eddie and I have wanted to quit and give up – how many times we have questioned if we really heard God or not. How many times we have felt like failures. But we must remain faithful! We must not despise small beginnings! Don't give up! Don't faint! Your miracle may be right around the corner!

Malachi 3:10 AMP
10 Bring all the tithes (the whole tenth of your
income) into the storehouse, that there may be food
in My house, and prove Me now by it, says the Lord
of hosts, if I will not open the windows of heaven for
you and pour you out a blessing, that there shall not
be room enough to receive it. [Malachi 2:2.]

While the ten virgins were waiting for the Bridegroom to come, they all fell asleep. At midnight a shout was heard "Behold, the bridegroom! Go out to meet him [Matthew 25:6]!" At once the ten virgins began to get their lamps in order to go and meet the Bridegroom. The foolish virgins said, "Please give us some of your oil [Anointing] because our lamps are going out." But the wise replied, "There will not be enough for us and for you; go instead to the dealers and buy for yourselves". This indicates that the five foolish virgins had the money [provision] to go and buy the oil but did not want to spend their money wisely by investing in the Anointing. They did not want to faithfully pay their tithes. According to Malachi 3:10, "tithe" means "tenth or tenth part".[9] They did not want to give offerings above their tithes. They just wanted to look like the "real deal"—like the five wise virgins. Robert Morris states in his book, <u>The Blessed Life</u>, pages 50-51, "What is true is that the number 10 is associated with testing throughout the Bible. And the tithe represents the ultimate 'heart test' for the believer. But, more significantly, tithing is also the only area in which the Christian is invited to test God." One of my brothers was sharing with me that on occasion he would be asked to help count the money that came in the church offering. He said, "I cannot tell you how many 'empty envelopes' were put in the offering baskets." Basically, people who wanted to "look like" they were giving in the offering—fakes and pretenders!

Eddie's Granny Powell used to say, "God does not always pay on Friday, but He always pays." That works for those who are wise and those who are foolish. When "payday" came, the five foolish virgins were exposed for who they really were. Remember, God had given the five foolish virgins the same provisions He had given to the wise virgins so there is no need to feel sorry for them!

Matthew 15:7-8 AMP
7 You pretenders (hypocrites)! Admirably and truly
did Isaiah prophesy of you when he said:
8 These people draw near Me with their mouths and
honor Me with their lips, but their hearts hold off
and are far away from Me.

The five wise virgins had chosen to be what God wanted them to be. The five wise virgins decided to say what God wanted them to say. The five wise virgins chose to be obedient to do what God wanted them to do. They were not quitters. They were prepared for their next assignment. The five wise virgins were honestly expecting the Bridegroom's return. They were the real deal! They had a lifestyle of faithfulness to the Anointing!

While the foolish virgins were going away to buy more oil, the bridegroom came. Those who were prepared went in with Him to the marriage feast and the door was shut. Later the other virgins came and said, "Lord, Lord, open [the door] to us!" But He replied, "I solemnly declare to you, I do not know you [I am not acquainted with you]." "Watch therefore [give strict attention and be cautious and active], for you know neither the day nor the hour when the Son of Man will come." God's warning applies to each and every one of us today. We need to be like the five wise virgins. We need to treat the Anointing as the sacred trust it is!

CHAPTER FOUR

KEY # 1 — GOD'S LOVE, THE FOUNDATIONAL KEY!

Matthew 22:37-40 AMP
37 And He replied to him, You shall love the Lord
your God with all your heart and with all your soul
and with all your mind (intellect).
38 This is the great (most important, principal) and
first commandment.
39 And a second is like it: You shall love your
neighbor as [you do] yourself.
40 These two commandments sum up and upon
them depend all the Law and the Prophets.

1 John 4:8 AMP
8 He who does not love has not become acquainted
with God [does not and never did know Him],
for God is love.

Hidden Motives of the Heart

Matthew 22:38 informs us that loving God with all our heart, soul, and mind is the most important commandment. We are operating in total disobedience when we function in the Anointing without loving God with all our heart, soul and mind. It is a total misuse of the Anointing!

The second most important commandment God has given us as believers is, "You shall love your neighbor as [you do] yourself." If you love others as you do yourself, you will not harm other people for your own exaltation.

The Bible tells us in I John 4:8 without love, we do not and never did know God, for God is Love! Operating in the Anointing power of God without knowing God is just like 1 Corinthians 13 states, "I am only a noisy gong or a clanging cymbal." Should we mistrust everyone who operates in God's Anointing because there are a few "noisy gongs and clanging cymbal's" out there? Absolutely not!

Therefore, we must make a point to make sure we know God and operate in His Love. We must ask ourselves, *"What is my heart's motive for moving in the Anointing or manifest power of God?"* We must be honest with ourselves! Is your motive to be the next hotshot in the "Who's Who in the Pentecostal Zoo"? Is your motive to receive the accolades of men and women? Is your motive to be admired and highly esteemed? Is your motive to receive financial gain? In Acts Chapter 8, we find an interesting character by the name of Simon, who amazed and dazzled the people with his skills in the magic arts. The people considered Simon great, extraordinary and distinguished. The people of Samaria paid earnest attention to him, from the least to the greatest, saying, "This man is the exhibition of the great power of God."

When Philip the Evangelist came to Samaria, these same people believed Philip's preaching about the Kingdom of God and the Name of Jesus Christ. All the men and women were baptized. Then Simon himself believed and was baptized into the Name of Jesus and began following Philip all around. Simon was amazed at the powerful signs and wonders performed by Philip.

The Apostles Peter and John were then sent to Samaria to pray for these same people to receive the Baptism in the Holy Spirit. As Peter and John laid hands on each one of them, the people were filled with the Holy Spirit. However, when Simon saw that the people received the Holy Spirit through Peter and John laying hands on the people, Simon offered Peter and John money, saying, "Grant me the power and authority so that anyone I lay hands on will receive the Holy Spirit."

Peter said, "May your money perish with you since you thought you could buy the 'free gift of God' with money! You have no part or share in this ministry because your heart is not right before God! Repent for this wickedness and pray that perhaps this thought of your heart may be forgiven you! For I see that you are poisoned by bitterness and bound by iniquity." Then Simon answered and said, "Pray to the Lord for me that none of the things that you have spoken will come upon me!"

Simon the sorcerer was not walking in the love of God. He was walking in a need for the admiration of others, a distinguished reputation. Simon was greedy for the money he thought he could gain from "using" the power of God.

Simon Versus Jesus Christ

Jesus Christ made of Himself no reputation! Jesus willingly laid down (gave) His life for you and me—even while we were yet sinners, the epitome of love [See John 10:18]! Jesus' motive was first and foremost LOVE. John 6:38 tells us Jesus did not come to earth to do His own will, but to fulfill and do the will of the Father. Jesus wanted to see people's hearts turn toward God. He wanted God to receive ALL the glory! Jesus made Himself of no reputation.

Is your motive to receive the accolades of men and women or is your motive to be like Jesus and do God's will

on the earth? Is your motive to bring and GIVE ALL THE
GLORY TO GOD? If so, you are on the right path! Is your
motive to see people's hearts turned toward God the Father,
God the Son and God the Holy Spirit? If so, follow Christ
Jesus' example!

Philippians 2:5-7 KJV
5 Let this mind be in you, which was also in Christ
Jesus: 6 Who, being in the form of God, thought
it not robbery to be equal with God: 7 But made
himself of no reputation, and took upon him the
form of a servant, and was made
in the likeness of men:

If you want a measuring stick for your love walk, read 1
Corinthians 13:1-8. We need a foundation of Love in order
to walk in God's Anointing because God is Love! Without
the love of God dwelling in us we are nothing but a noisy
gong or a clanging cymbal!

1 Corinthians 13:1-8 AMP
1 IF I [can] speak in the tongues of men and
[even] of angels, but have not love (that reasoning,
intentional, spiritual devotion such as is inspired by
God's love for and in us), I am only a
noisy gong or a clanging cymbal.
2 And if I have prophetic powers (the gift of
interpreting the divine will and purpose), and
understand all the secret truths and mysteries and
possess all knowledge, and if I have [sufficient]
faith so that I can remove mountains, but have not
love (God's love in me) I am nothing
(a useless nobody).
3 Even if I dole out all that I have [to the poor in
providing] food, and if I surrender my body to be

*burned or in order that I may glory, but have not
love (God's love in me), I gain nothing.
4 Love endures long and is patient and kind; love
never is envious nor boils over with jealousy, is not
boastful or vainglorious,
does not display itself haughtily.
5 It is not conceited (arrogant and inflated with
pride); it is not rude (unmannerly) and does not
act unbecomingly. Love (God's love in us) does not
insist on its own rights or its own way, for it is not
self-seeking; it is not touchy or fretful or resentful;
it takes no account of the evil done to it [it pays no
attention to a suffered wrong].
6 It does not rejoice at injustice and
unrighteousness, but rejoices
when right and truth prevail.
7 Love bears up under anything and everything
that comes, is ever ready to believe the best of
every person, its hopes are fadeless under all
circumstances, and it endures everything
[without weakening].
8 Love never fails [never fades out or becomes
obsolete or comes to an end]. As for prophecy (the
gift of interpreting the divine will and purpose),
it will be fulfilled and pass away; as for tongues,
they will be destroyed and cease; as for knowledge,
it will pass away [it will lose its value and be
superseded by truth].*

Worker of Iniquity

*Matthew 7:22-23 KJV
22 Many will say to me in that day, Lord, Lord, have
we not prophesied in thy name? and in thy name
have cast out devils? and in thy name*

done many wonderful works?
23 And then will I profess unto them, I never knew
you: depart from me, ye that work iniquity.

A person can learn to operate in God's Anointing and not walk in God's love. Any person who operates in God's Anointing and does not walk in God's love is also a "Worker of Iniquity". This is why God said, "Depart from Me, you who work iniquity."

Spirit Versus Flesh

Galatians 3:3 AMP
3 Are you so foolish and so senseless and so silly?
Having begun [your new life spiritually] with the
[Holy] Spirit, are you now reaching perfection [by
dependence] on the flesh?

One trap some people fall into after having a great beginning with God, they forget their foundation of love and fall into operating in the flesh. These people earnestly start out right, but when the demands come to "perform" and God hasn't sanctioned a "performance", they begin to rely on the flesh, which can only lead to operating in a satanic realm. Some get used to the accolades and give in to "having to look good" in the eyes of men. Whatever the reason, we must all guard our hearts. It is never wise to think you are above falling into temptation! In fact, when we think we can never fall into temptation, we are already on a slippery slope to failure!

It is imperative that each and every one of us maintains our love walk with God, Who is Love! Maintaining our love walk with God is the only way we can truly love people and keep our hearts pure! You can fool some people for a while, but God always sees the motives of our heart. In the light of eternity, looking like a hot shot down here on earth is not only shallow, but also foolish. It can become very dangerous as Simon found out! Let's be honest, is anything worse then hearing God say, "Depart from me I never knew you"? To spend eternity in hell for a few fleeting moments of power and recognition here on earth is not a path anyone should choose!

Tragically, not only will the "Simons" of this world live eternally in Hell if they do not repent, but many people who have been injured by an "acclaimed man or woman of God" will also live eternally in Hell! The cost to the Kingdom because of the failure of acclaimed leaders to maintain their love walk with God is eternally expensive.

CHAPTER FIVE

Key # 2 — WE NEED TO BE CHRIST LIKE!

Romans 8:29 AMP
29 For those whom He foreknew [of whom He was
aware and loved beforehand], He also destined
from the beginning [foreordaining them] to be
molded into the image of His Son [and share
inwardly His likeness], that He might become the
firstborn among many brethren.

R omans 8:29 informs us that God destined us from the beginning to be molded into the image of Jesus Christ His Son. When people look at us, they should see Christ in us the hope of glory [Colossians 1:27].

Matthew 1:16 AMP
16 Jacob the father of Joseph, the husband of Mary,
of whom was born Jesus, Who is called the Christ.
(The Messiah, the Anointed).

Acts 10:38 AMP
38 How God anointed and consecrated Jesus of
Nazareth with the [Holy] Spirit and with strength
and ability and power; how He went about doing
good and, in particular, curing all who were
harassed and oppressed by [the power of] the devil,
for God was with Him.

In Matthew 1:16, Jesus was given two distinct names, "Jesus" and "Christ". Jesus Christ was fully man and fully God. In Acts 10:38 the Bible tells us how God anointed and consecrated *"Jesus of Nazareth" — the human "man" part of Jesus Christ*—with the Holy Spirit and with strength and ability and power. Since *Christ is "The Messiah, The Anointed One" —the God part of Jesus Christ*, there was no need for the "Christ" part to be anointed! Kenneth and Gloria Copeland have been known to aptly say it this way on television, "Jesus Christ the Anointed One and His Anointing."

To be "Christ-like" is to be dependent upon The Anointed One and His Anointing. This means that we being *fully man anointed by God* will go about doing good and in particular, curing all who are harassed and oppressed by the power of the devil, for God is with us! In fact *if Jesus, the "man" had to be anointed by God and Jesus is just as much man as He is God, then how much more do you and I need to be anointed by God!*

Acts 10:38 tells us that after Jesus was anointed, He went around *doing* good and curing all who were harassed and oppressed by the power of the devil, for God was with Him. Jesus not only received a *"touch* of God's Anointing", but Jesus allowed God's Anointing "touch" to go down deep inside of Him to *change* Him into what God wanted Him to be and then Jesus allowed God's "touch" or "the Anointing" to flow through Him to *touch and change* His world by doing good—curing all who were harassed and oppressed by the power of the devil. This means that Jesus did not just bask "in the Presence" or in the "feelings" of the Anointing He received. Jesus allowed the Anointing to go deep down inside of Him to change him into what God intended Him to be. Then Jesus *acted* upon the Anointing by going around doing good—healing the sick and setting the captives free!

> *Luke 4:18-21 AMP*
> *18 The Spirit of the Lord [is] upon Me, because He*
> *has anointed Me [the Anointed one, the Messiah]*
> *to preach the good news (the Gospel) to the poor;*
> *He has sent Me to announce release to the captives*
> *and recovery of sight to the blind, to send forth*
> *as delivered those who are oppressed [who are*
> *downtrodden, bruised, crushed,*
> *and broken down by calamity],*
> *19 To proclaim the accepted and acceptable year of*
> *the Lord [the day when salvation and the free favors*
> *of God profusely abound.] [Isaiah 61:1,2.]*
> *20 Then He rolled up the book and gave it back to*
> *the attendant and sat down; and the eyes of all in*
> *the synagogue were gazing [attentively] at Him.*
> *21 And He began to speak to them: Today this*
> *Scripture has been fulfilled while*
> *you are present and hearing.*

Jesus' ministry began when He was about 30 years old. In Luke chapter three, John the Baptist baptized Jesus in water. The Holy Spirit led Jesus into the wilderness for 40 days of testing. After passing the tests, Jesus full of and under the power of the Holy Spirit, goes back to Nazareth where He was born and goes to the Synagogue, as was His custom. Jesus then reads Isaiah 61:1-2 and informs them that He is the fulfillment of the scripture. He is the Anointed One. This is the passage that God used to call me into the ministry.

Ever since I can remember, I had a sense of being called into the ministry. In the spring of 1984, it seemed like every time I turned around someone would quote this passage and the Anointing would come all over me. The Holy Spirit would tell me that I was called into the ministry to do just what Isaiah 61:1-2 and Luke 4:18-19 said.

Because

Isaiah 61:1-4 AMP
*1 THE SPIRIT of the Lord God is upon me, **because** the Lord has anointed and qualified me to preach the Gospel of good tidings to the meek, the poor, and afflicted; He has sent me to bind up and heal the brokenhearted, to proclaim liberty to the [physical and spiritual] captives and the opening of the prison and of the eyes to those who are bound, [Romans 10:15.]*
2 To proclaim the acceptable year of the Lord [the year of His favor] and the day of vengeance of our God, to comfort all who mourn,
[Matthew 11:2-6; Luke 4:18,19; 7:22.]
3 To grant [consolation and joy] to those who mourn in Zion—to give them an ornament (a garland or diadem) of beauty instead of ashes, the oil of joy instead of mourning, the garment [expressive] of praise instead of a heavy, burdened, and failing spirit—that they may be called oaks of righteousness [lofty, strong, and magnificent, distinguished for uprightness, justice, and right standing with God], the planting of the Lord, that He may be glorified.
4 And they shall rebuild the ancient ruins; they shall raise up the former desolations and renew the ruined cities, the devastations of many generations.

Notice in Isaiah 61:1 and Luke 4:18 "The Spirit of the Lord God is upon me *BECAUSE*"! This tells us that God's "Anointing" or "manifested Presence" comes upon us for a reason! Although it is wonderful to lay and bask in the Presence of God, the reason is not to just have a party. I don't want anyone to think that I am against the "party" part of the Anointing. Just the contrary, I myself love to lay and soak in His Presence. Many times in the party setting, God has been doing surgery on me –showing me areas where I need to change. While I am under the Anointing, God is able to show me things that might otherwise crush me. It is not painful. It is refreshing! Many other people have shared that they also have had the same experience where God has dealt with a painful issue while they were laying on the floor laughing. They, too, did not feel any pain, but they felt released and refreshed. The reason this has happened to us is that we allowed God to come in us and change us. While under the party Anointing, I have received instructions, revelation, and much more. Just like Isaiah 61 says, many of us have had God bind up and heal our broken hearts!

Isaiah 61 goes on to tell us the many reasons the Anointing comes upon a person:

- To preach the Gospel
- To bind up and heal the brokenhearted
- To proclaim liberty to the captives
- To proclaim the acceptable year of the Lord –the year of His favor and the day of vengeance of our God
- To comfort all who mourn
- To grant joy to all who mourn – the oil of joy instead of mourning
- To give people beauty instead of ashes
- To give the garment of praise instead of a heavy, burdened and failing spirit

In fact, the entire chapter of Isaiah 61 tells us about the other things the Anointing does. For instance you will receive double for your trouble. I would encourage you to stop and read the entire chapter of Isaiah 61. Allow the Holy Spirit to not only touch you, but to change you. Then go forth to touch and change the world.

Greater Things

John 14:12 AMP
12 I assure you, most solemnly I tell you, if anyone
steadfastly believes in Me, he will himself be able to
do the things that I do; and he will do even greater
things than these, because I go to the Father.

How can we possibly do greater things than Jesus did? Jesus raised the dead! Jesus controlled the weather by telling a storm to be quiet and the hurricane force winds ceased at His word. Jesus walked on the water and had Peter out there walking with Him. When Peter began to sink; Jesus saved him from drowning and put Peter back in the boat.

Many discussions have been made over what Jesus meant by, "he will do even greater things than these". There is one thing of which I am sure, neither you nor I will do even the same things Jesus did nor "the greater things" if we are not "anointed" by the Holy Spirit! Think about it, Peter's shadow began healing people because the Anointing of God was so powerfully working through him! I don't know about you, but to my knowledge to date, my shadow has not healed anyone. The great news is that all things are possible with God [Matthew 19:26]! We just need to listen and obey!

The Love/Hate Response

After Jesus informs the people that He is the fulfillment of the scripture in Luke 4:21, He received varied responses. Generally, when you walk in God's Anointing, people either love you or they want to kill you. One minute the people were speaking well of Jesus and then the next minute those same people said, "Isn't this Joseph's son?" or in other words, "Who does Jesus think He is?"

Just a couple of verses later, Jesus states, "A prophet is without honor in his own town." Finally, those same people who spoke well of Jesus decided they were going to kill Jesus by pushing him off a cliff [Luke 4:22-29]. Walking in the Anointing may literally cost you your very life.

1 Peter 4:12-13 NIV
12 Dear friends, do not be surprised at the painful
trial you are suffering, as though something strange
were happening to you. 13 But rejoice that you
participate in the sufferings of Christ, so that you
may be overjoyed when his glory is revealed.

Peter and John experienced the "Love/Hate" response while operating under the Anointing of the Holy Spirit. In Acts chapters three and four, Peter and John were going up to the temple at three o'clock in the afternoon. A forty plus year old man crippled from birth, sat at the gate of the temple, which is called Beautiful to beg for charitable gifts. He asked Peter and John to give him a gift. Peter and John intently looked at him and said, "Look at us!" The crippled man looked at them expecting to get money from them. Peter told the crippled man, "I do not have money, but what I do have I give to you; in the Name of Jesus Christ of Nazareth, walk!" Then Peter took hold of the man's right hand with a firm grip and raised him up. At once the crippled man's feet and anklebones became strong and steady! The man not only began to walk, but he began to leap and praise God before all the people. The people recognized him as the man who usually sat begging at the Beautiful Gate of the temple. They were filled with wonder and amazement! The crowds started to gather around Peter, John and the healed man at Solomon's Porch. Peter began to explain to the people that neither he nor John healed this man.

Acts 3:13-17 AMP
3 The God of Abraham and of Isaac and of Jacob,
the God of our forefathers, has glorified His Servant
and Son Jesus [doing Him this honor], Whom you
indeed delivered up and denied and rejected and
disowned in the presence of Pilate, when he had
determined to let Him go.
14 But you denied and rejected and disowned the
Pure and Holy, the Just and Blameless one, and
demanded [the pardon of]
a murderer to be granted to you.
15 But you killed the very Source (the Author) of
life, Whom God raised from the dead.
To this we are witnesses.
16 And His name, through and by faith in His name,
has made this man whom you see and recognize
well and strong. [Yes] the faith which is through
and by Him [Jesus] has given the man this perfect
soundness [of body] before all of you.
17 And now, brethren, I know that you acted in
ignorance [not aware of what you were doing], as
did your rulers also.

While Peter and John continued talking to the people, the high priests and the military commander of the temple and the Sadducees came upon them. They were livid that

Peter and John were teaching about Jesus and His resurrection from the dead. So they arrested Peter and John and put them in prison.

The Next Day

Acts 4:7, 8, 13 AMP
7 And they set the men in their midst and repeatedly
demanded, By what sort of power or by what kind of
authority did [such people as]
you do this [healing]?
8 Then Peter, [because he was] filled with [and
controlled by] the Holy Spirit, said to them, Rulers
of the people and members of the council
(the Sanhedrin),
13 Now when they saw the boldness and unfettered
eloquence of Peter and John and perceived that
they were unlearned and untrained in the schools
[common men with no educational advantages],
they marveled; and they recognized
that they had been with Jesus.

Just as people marveled and recognized that Peter and John had been with Jesus, people will marvel and recognize that you have been with Jesus when you walk in the Anointing"! After being touched and changed so mightily in 1993 by the Anointing, Eddie and I regularly had people stare at us and say they saw a light all around us. We were doing a revival in Clinton, Maryland and a little girl drew a picture and handed it to us. It was a picture of Eddie and me doing Praise and Worship. There was a golden light emanating all around us. When I asked the little girl about the golden light in the picture, she said she drew what she saw. Does that make Eddie or me something special? No! It is Jesus spilling out of us that people see! I am telling you that the Anointing will turn you into another man/woman! You will walk differently. You will talk differently! You will behave differently! You will speak with authority when you are under the Anointing. People will perceive that you have been with Jesus! You will be conformed into the image of Christ.

Peter and John had to be set free from prison. There wasn't anything Peter and John's accusers could say in opposition, since they saw the man who had been cured standing there beside them. Peter and John were let go with a warning that they were not to converse or teach at all about the Name of Jesus. Peter and John replied to them, "You judge whether it is right for us to obey you rather than to listen and obey God. We must speak what God tells us to speak." Peter and John were further threatened and let go. Many of the people who heard Peter and John's message became believers in Jesus as the Christ! And the Christians grew in number to about 5,000. People will either love or hate you when you walk in the Anointing. People will come to believe in Jesus as the Christ when you walk in the Anointing!

When the people get filled to overflowing in the Anointing and begin being His disciples, I firmly believe that pastors will be bailing some of their parishioners out of jail for healing people in the Name of Jesus in the marketplace! The opposite will also be true. Some of the parishioners will be bailing out their pastors.

Prayer—A Time To Sit And Soak

After being set free from prison, Peter and John returned to prayer. Peter and John had the wisdom to realize that they needed to be refilled, refueled, and refreshed before taking the enemy on again! Here is what they prayed:

Acts 4:29-33 AMP
29 And now, Lord, observe their threats and grant
to Your bond servants [full freedom]
to declare Your message fearlessly,
30 While You stretch out Your hand to cure and to
perform signs and wonders through the authority
and by the power of the name of
Your holy Child and Servant Jesus.
31 And when they had prayed, the place in which
they were assembled was shaken; and they were all
filled with the Holy Spirit, and they continued to
speak the Word of God with freedom
and boldness and courage.
32 Now the company of believers was of one heart
and soul, and not one of them claimed that anything
which he possessed was [exclusively] his own, but
everything they had was in common and
for the use of all.
33 And with great strength and ability and power
the apostles delivered their testimony to the
resurrection of the Lord Jesus, and great grace
(loving-kindness and favor and goodwill)
rested richly upon them all.

After prayer, the place they were in was shaken. They
were *all filled* with the Holy Spirit. They continued to speak
the Word of God with freedom and boldness and courage,
just like the Day of Pentecost. They did not go forward
without a fresh Pentecost!

We must be refilled and filled again and filled again and
filled again! Notice that once the apostles and believers were
filled with the Holy Spirit they manifested freedom, boldness, courage, as well as great strength, ability, power and
the Anointing to speak about Jesus! We must continually be
being filled!

Matthew 18:19-20 AMP
19 Again I tell you, if two of you on earth agree
(harmonize together, make a symphony together)
about whatever [anything and everything] they may
ask, it will come to pass and be done for them by
My Father in heaven.
20 For wherever two or three are gathered (drawn
together as My followers) in (into) My name, there I
AM in the midst of them.

It is very important whom you hang out with! There are people who will steal your joy. There are people who will try and steal your Anointing. There are people who will encourage you to pull away from God and His Anointing! There are people who are sent from the enemy to be a distraction to you. You need to pray and hang out with like-minded people! There is power in agreement! Unfortunately, there is power in agreement for good or bad! Choose life!

Acts 13:50-52 AMP
50 But the Jews stirred up the devout women of
high rank and the outstanding men of the town, and
instigated persecution against Paul and Barnabas
and drove them out of their boundaries. 51 But [the
apostles] shook off the dust from their feet against
them and went to Iconium. 52 And the disciples
were continually filled [throughout their souls] with
joy and the Holy Spirit.

Sometimes we need to "shake the dust from our feet". When God sends you somewhere to share the gospel and the people refuse to receive what God has sent you to deposit, shake the dust off your feet and move on to the next assignment. Do not let people's rejection of the Anointing deposited in you cause you to walk away from the Anointing!

Walk away from them! There are people waiting for you to arrive and display the Love of God to them! Do not let the enemy of our soul use naysayers and those in opposition to discourage you from your destiny! Even Jesus stood over Jerusalem frustrated because the people would not let Him bring them life [Luke 13:34].

Having A Life Worth Living

God intends for us to follow Jesus' pattern by allowing, "the Anointing" to not only "flow to us to touch us" and "flow in us to change us", but to allow His Anointing to continuously flow through us to touch and change our world! Consequently, Jesus' life is still impacting and touching the world today. So can our lives as we submit to the work of the Anointing to go down deep inside of us and change us so we can change our world! We must recognize that Jesus is the Anointer and we are the anointed.

So many people choose to stay at the "I will only allow the Anointing of the Holy Spirit to come upon me or touch me. I just want the party. I don't want to change. I'm not really hungry for more of God. It may cost me something." So much for "Well done, My good and faithful servant"! I believe this selfish party spirit goes along with the wicked and lazy servant [See Matthew 25:23-30].

The upside of being Christ-like by allowing the Anointing of God to flow through us to touch and change other's lives, is a life of true righteousness, peace and joy in the Holy Ghost—having a life worth living!

CHAPTER SIX

KEY #3 — WE MUST BE A PERSON OF GODLY CHARACTER IN ORDER TO MAINTAIN THE ANOINTING –PART 1

We must be a person of Godly character in order to maintain the Anointing. The Anointing will only take you as far as your character allows. God was always the "King of Israel", but the people began crying out for a "King" like the other nations had, so He gave them King Saul. God's choice was to rule the people through His appointed judges with Himself being their King [See I Samuel 8]. Since the Israelites rejected God as their King [1 Samuel 10:19], God instructed the Prophet Samuel to "Anoint" Saul for the office of King.

Samuel Anoints Saul
What were the "results" of Samuel's Anointing Saul?

1 Samuel 10:1, 6-7 & 9-11 AMP
*1 THEN SAMUEL took the vial of oil and poured it
on Saul's head and kissed him and said, has not the
Lord <u>anointed</u> you to be prince over
His heritage Israel?*
*6 Then the Spirit of the Lord will come upon you
mightily, and you will show yourself to be a prophet
with them; and you will be turned into another man.*
*7 When these signs meet you, do whatever you find
to be done, for God is with you.*
*9 And when [Saul] had turned his back to leave
Samuel, God gave him another heart, and all these
signs came to pass that day.*
*10 When they came to the hill [Gibeah], behold,
a band of prophets met him; and the Spirit of God
came mightily upon him, and he spoke under divine
inspiration among them.*
*11 And when all who knew Saul before saw that
he spoke by inspiration among the [schooled]
prophets, the people said one to another, What has
come over [him, who is nobody but] the son of
Kish? Is Saul also among the prophets?*

We just read five tangible real life results Saul received
from being anointed by God!

*   Saul was turned into another man [1 Samuel 10:6,
    21-24].
*   Whatever Saul found to be done, God promised to be
    with Saul [1 Samuel 10:7].
*   God gave Saul another heart [1 Samuel 10:9].

- The Spirit of the Lord came upon him mightily = empowerment [1 Samuel 10:10].
- Saul showed himself to be a prophet [1 Samuel 10:10-11].

The Anointing perceptibly changes people. In Acts chapter two, the 120 in the Upper Room became bold and extremely effective in soul winning immediately after being "anointed" and filled with the Holy Spirit. They also became very generous, selling what they had and giving to those in need. It appears to me that the 120 people in the Upper Room also received a "new heart"! The Apostle Peter cursed and denied he knew Jesus fifty days prior to the Upper Room experience, yet on the day of the outpouring of the Holy Spirit, he BOLDLY preaches and some 3,000 people are saved! There are differing levels of the Anointing and that level of Anointing determines if you have a short-lived change of heart or a life-long change of heart!

God is looking for people of Godly character — people with moral fiber! Saul did not remain in the Anointing, but was full of PRIDE, LYING, REBELLION and DISOBEDIENCE. He cared more about what "the PEOPLE" thought than what God thought – all character breakers! You and I can experience the Anointing, but the Anointing can only take us as far as our moral fiber takes us.

King Saul's Moral Failures

Let us take a look at the moral failures that plagued King Saul and plagues people today. So many times we think of a moral failure as adultery. Adultery is definitely a moral failure; it is not the only one. God intends for us to be people of integrity, honor, and honesty and ethically sound. Moral failure and the Anointing cannot coexist. Sin will not only disqualify you from walking in the Anointing, but will cause you to lose the Anointing!

Pride

Pride caused King Saul to lie and be disobedient to God in order to please the people. I Samuel 15:12 tells us that Saul set up a monument to himself and his victory. What happened to Saul? When he was to be presented to the people as their first King, Saul went and hid among the baggage [1 Samuel 10: 21-24]. What a swing of the pendulum! Saul, who hid from the people, now erects a monument to himself and his victory! A true man or woman of God would have erected a monument to God for giving the victory to them!

The Bible tells us in Philippians 2:3-13 not to think too highly of ourselves, but to be like Jesus. The same thing could happen to us if we forget God is the one who anoints and appoints. We are just earthen vessels to be used by God!

Second Corinthians 4:7 tells us that we have this treasure in earthen vessels that the excellency of the power may be of Him and not of ourselves. It is God's power and plan working through us. We are the gloves and God is the hand in the glove! God's Anointing is a sacred trust. We must always be mindful to give God the glory!

Lying

1 Samuel 15:13
"And Samuel came to Saul, and Saul said to him, Blessed are you of the Lord. I have performed what the Lord ordered. 14 And Samuel said, What then means this bleating of the sheep in my ears, and the lowing of the oxen which I hear?"

Saul obviously did not destroy ALL. Saul lies again in 1 Samuel 15:20-21 with verse 21 starting with a big old "BUT". With God, let your yes be yes and your no be no [James 5:12]. In fact one of the Ten Commandments is "Do not lie" [Matthew 19:18]. You cannot be a person of moral fiber or a person of character if you are a liar. The Holy Spirit will only deal with you for a time and then your lies will be revealed. The Anointing and lying cannot continue to dwell together.

The Blame Game

1 Samuel 15:15 AMP
15 Saul said, They have brought them from the Amalekites; for the people spared the best of the sheep and oxen to sacrifice to the Lord your God, but the rest we have utterly destroyed.

The Blame Game goes all the way back to the Garden of Eden…it was this woman you gave me…it was the serpent [Genesis 3:12-13]. King Saul told Samuel the Prophet that *it was the people who spared the best of the animals to sacrifice to "your God"* [emphasis mine]. Not only was King Saul playing the Blame Game, he was lying. In order to be a person of moral fiber and of good character, we must take responsibility for our own actions. People who cannot admit that they are ever wrong never grow up. They miss out of many great relationships with others. After all you can never resolve a problem if you cannot admit to being wrong. At best, your relationships are stunted, especially your relationship with God.

King David blew it big time by committing murder and adultery, but he *did not* blame anyone else but himself. He admitted that he had sinned against God [2 Samuel 12:13]. The big difference between King Saul and King David was

King David's admitting his sin and taking responsibility for his own sin. It is the reason David was not removed from the throne. In order to maintain the Anointing, we must keep a clean slate with God. It is as easy as:

1 John 1:9-10 AMP
9 If we [freely] admit that we have sinned and confess our sins, He is faithful and just (true to His own nature and promises) and will forgive our sins [dismiss our lawlessness] and [continuously] cleanse us from all unrighteousness [everything not in conformity to His will in purpose, thought, and action].
10 If we say (claim) we have not sinned, we contradict His Word and make Him out to be false and a liar, and His Word is not in us [the divine message of the Gospel is not in our hearts].

Knowing God

Daniel 11:32 AMP
32 And such as violate the covenant he shall pervert and seduce with flatteries, but the people who know their God shall prove themselves strong and shall stand firm and do exploits [for God].

King Saul also had a problem in that he did not know God for himself. He only had a secondhand relationship with God through the Prophet Samuel and called God, "the Lord your God".

You are robbing both you and God when you only have a secondhand relationship with God. Basically, a secondhand relationship is no relationship! Instead of allowing the Anointing to go in him to change him and then allowing that same Anointing to flow through him to touch and change the world around him, King Saul only allowed the Anointing to come "upon" him. Anyone can receive a "touch" from the Anointing or the manifest Presence of God. However, if that manifest Presence of God is not allowed to flow into a person to change that person and then flow through that same person to touch and change the world around them, it becomes nothing more than a one-time experience instead of a life changing experience. This secondhand relationship is another big difference between King Saul and King David! David knew God firsthand!

David Is Anointed King

King David was anointed King in I Samuel 16. The Prophet Samuel was sent to the House of Jesse to anoint one of Jesse's sons King in place of King Saul. Jesse brought seven of his sons to Samuel to let Samuel determine which son was to be anointed King, but Samuel said, "None of these seven are to be anointed King. Do you have another son?" The youngest son, David, who was still a boy, was out tending the sheep. Neither Jesse nor David's older brothers even considered that God would choose to Anoint David, King! When David came in from tending the sheep, God instructed Samuel to arise and Anoint David. The Bible tells us that the Spirit came mightily upon David from that day forward. David did not ask for a crown and a scepter. The wonderful thing about David versus Saul, is that David just went back to tending his sheep and worshipping God.

King David Knew God

David had a firsthand relationship with God! One day [1 Samuel 17], David's father, Jesse asked David to go and check on his three oldest brothers who had joined with King Saul's army and bring them some food. While David was asking his brother's how they were doing, Goliath, the champion, the Philistine of Gath came forth as he had the previous forty days and *David heard him:*

1 Samuel 17:8-11 AMP
Goliath stood and shouted to the ranks of Israel,
Why have you come out to draw up for battle? Am
I not a Philistine, and are you not servants of Saul?
Choose a man for yourselves and
let him come down to me.
9 If he is able to fight with me and kill me, then we
will be your servants; but if I prevail against him
and kill him, then you shall be
our servants and serve us.
10 And the Philistine said, I defy the ranks of Israel
this day; give me a man, that we may fight together.
11 When Saul and all Israel heard those words of
the Philistine, they were dismayed
and greatly afraid.

Now all of the Israelites including King Saul heard what Goliath was saying and they were terrified. They obviously did not have a "firsthand knowledge of God" because *David "heard" the real message from Goliath—Goliath was defying God!*

1 Samuel 17:26 AMP
"And David said to the men standing by him, What
shall be done for the man who kills this Philistine
and takes away the reproach from Israel? For who
is this uncircumcised Philistine that he should defy
the armies of the living God?"

When King Saul got wind of what David said, King Saul called for David. David's brothers were angry with David.

They thought he was just trying to get a look at the battle-field and tried to stop him.

The Bible keeps referring to David as an adolescent. In the Jewish community boys are considered to be a man at the age of thirteen. David could have possibly been only twelve years old. Goliath on the other hand was about 10 feet tall and was wearing heavy armor – the weight is unknown.

King Saul encourages David to wear King Saul's armor. David tried it on, but it was not the right size and David was not accustomed to it. There is a big lesson here. Once God anoints us, we need to try and avoid well-meaning people who will try to get us to do things "their way" or to possibly use what works for them. Eddie and I had well meaning people tell us that there was no way that we could do the Praise and Worship portion of the service and preach. First of all, God told us to and anointed us to minister in praise and worship and in the preaching of the Word. Secondly, we must obey God, not man! We need to let God use us in the manner He has always used us. In David's case it was using the same anointed tools he did as a shepherd boy – five smooth stones and a slingshot. Little becomes much in God's hands! After all how could David lose when he was standing up for the living God with Whom David had a firsthand relationship? The same God had helped him kill a lion and then a bear that were after the sheep David was tending.

1 Samuel 17:43-51 AMP
43 And the Philistine said to David, Am I a dog,
that you should come to me with sticks? And the
Philistine cursed David by his gods.
44 The Philistine said to David, Come to me, and I
will give your flesh to the birds
of the air and the beasts of the field.
45 Then said David to the Philistine, You come to
me with a sword, a spear, and a javelin, but I come

*to you in the name of the Lord of hosts, the God of
the ranks of Israel, Whom you have defied.
46 This day the Lord will deliver you into my hand,
and I will smite you and cut off your head. And I
will give the corpses of the army of the Philistines
this day to the birds of the air and the wild beasts of
the earth, that all the earth may
know that there is a God in Israel.
47 And all this assembly shall know that the Lord
saves not with sword and spear; for* the battle is the
Lord's, *and He will give you into our hands.
48 When the Philistine came forward to meet David,
David ran quickly toward the battle
line to meet the Philistine.
49 David put his hand into his bag and took out
a stone and slung it, and it struck the Philistine,
sinking into his forehead, and he fell
on his face to the earth.
50 So David prevailed over the Philistine with
a sling and with a stone, and struck down the
Philistine and slew him.
But no sword was in David's hand.
51 So he ran and stood over the Philistine, took his
sword and drew it out of its sheath, and killed him,
and cut off his head with it. When the Philistines
saw that their mighty champion was dead, they fled.*

There are several notable things in this passage:

- God used Goliath's own words against him. In verse
  44 The Philistine said to David, "Come to me, and
  I will give your flesh to the birds of the air and the
  beasts of the field". David not only gave Goliath's
  flesh to the birds of the air and the beasts of the field,

but the Philistine Armies' flesh to the birds of the air and the beasts of the field! Go God! Go David!

• In verse 48, when Goliath started forward to meet David, David ran quickly toward the battle line. NO FEAR HERE!

• David used Goliath's sword to chop Goliath's head off [Verse 51]!

If you read further, the Israelites defeated the Philistine Army and plundered their tents. Total victory! Who knows if your knowing God and operating in the Anointing of God will cause others to rise up and take their rightful place?

Fear of Man

Proverbs 29:25 AMP
25 The fear of man brings a snare, but whoever leans on, trusts in, and puts his confidence in the Lord is safe and set on high.

I Samuel 15: 24 says that King Saul feared what he looked like to the people and obeyed their voice. Once again look at the difference between King Saul and King David! David stood up for God against his brothers' heckling and Goliath's fearsome body and threats! David stood up to the King and would not give in by wearing the armor that the King wanted him to wear. David was only concerned with pleasing and avenging God!

The only being you and I need to please is God the Father, God the Son and God the Holy Spirit!

CHAPTER SEVEN

KEY #3—WE MUST BE A PERSON OF GODLY CHARACTER IN ORDER TO MAINTAIN THE ANOINTING PART 2

1 Thessalonians 5:19-24 AMP
19 Do not quench (suppress or subdue)
the [Holy] Spirit;
20 Do not spurn the gifts and utterances of the
prophets [do not depreciate prophetic revelations
nor despise inspired instruction
or exhortation or warning].
21 But test and prove all things [until you can
recognize] what is good; [to that] hold fast.
22 Abstain from evil [shrink from it and keep aloof
from it] in whatever form or
whatever kind it may be.
23 And may the God of peace Himself sanctify you
through and through [separate you from profane
things, make you pure and wholly consecrated

*to God]; and may **your spirit and soul and body***
[Emphasis mine] be preserved sound and complete
[and found] blameless at the coming of our Lord
Jesus Christ (the Messiah).
24 Faithful is He Who is calling you [to Himself]
and utterly trustworthy, and He will also do it
[fulfill His call by hallowing and keeping you].

1 Corinthians 14:18 AMP
18 I thank God that I speak in [strange] tongues
(languages) more than any of you or
all of you put together;

From the beginning we were created to be a spirit man living in a physical body, having a natural experience. Since sin entered into the picture, we keep acting as though we are natural beings having a spiritual experience. We must begin to once again listen to our spirit man until it overrules our natural carnal man/mind! It is possible. The more you purpose to listen to the Holy Spirit within you, the louder His voice becomes! I will give you a little secret. Pray in tongues, in the Holy Spirit, as much as possible every day! It will keep you in touch with your spirit man. That is why Paul said in First Corinthians, "I thank God that I speak in tongues more than any of you all put together." The only way Paul could have made this statement and be honest was to pray in tongues at every opportunity. Paul knew the power of speaking in tongues! Paul knew speaking in tongues would keep his heart right before God. Paul knew that speaking in tongues would keep his spirit man in first place.

Samson Did Not Honor or Esteem The Anointing

A woman or man of Godly character will honor and esteem the Anointing! We must be willing to pay the price for the Anointing! It would be best at this time to read Judges chapter thirteen through sixteen before proceeding.

Judges 13:2-5, 24-25 AMP
2 And there was a certain man of Zorah, of the tribe of the Danites, whose name was Manoah; and his wife was barren and had no children.
3 And the Angel of the Lord appeared to the woman and said to her, Behold, you are barren and have no children, but you shall become pregnant and bear a son.
4 Therefore beware and drink no wine or strong drink and eat nothing unclean.
5 For behold, you shall become pregnant and bear a son. No razor shall come upon his head, for the child shall be a **Nazirite to God from birth***, and he shall begin to deliver Israel out of the hands of the Philistines.*
24 And the woman [in due time] bore a son and called his name Samson; and the child grew and the Lord blessed him.
25 And the Spirit of the Lord began to move him at times in Mahaneh-dan [the camp of Dan] between Zorah and Eshtaol.

What Is A Nazirite Vow?

The Bible tells us the rules for a woman or man taking what it called "A Nazirite Vow" in Numbers 6:1-21. One of the rules was they were not to put a razor to her/his head. Samson's distinction from other people who took the Nazirite Vow was that the secret to his supernatural strength was that he had never had a razor taken to his hair. The other's who had taken a Nazirite Vow did not possess supernatural strength.

Samson's supernatural strength was the Anointing—"and the Spirit of the Lord, came mightily upon him".

Judges 14:5-6, 19 AMP
5 Then Samson and his father and mother went down to Timnah and came to the vineyards of Timnah. And behold, a young lion roared against him. 6 And the Spirit of the Lord came mightily upon him, and he tore the lion as he would have torn a kid, and he had nothing in his hand; but he did not tell his father or mother what he had done. 19 And the Spirit of the Lord came upon him, and he went down to Ashkelon and slew thirty men of them and took their apparel [as spoil], and gave the changes of garments to those who explained the riddle. And his anger was kindled, and he went up to his father's house.

Samson would bring to mind the image of Atlas—the one who is lifting the entire world on his shoulders or the image of a Mr. America or the cartoon character "The Hulk". Samson had supernatural strength given to him by the Lord to defeat the Philistines—"And the Spirit of the Lord came upon him". That supernatural strength is the Anointing or manifest Presence of God.

Samson, however, did not *honor nor esteem the Anointing* of the Holy Spirit! He evidently took it for granted. Bad choice! He made a lot of other bad choices. He had a weakness that he chose not to overcome—he had a thing for the Philistine women. If you read the entire story of Samson, you will see that God gave Samson time to repent, but Samson repeatedly chose to live a sinful life until God's longsuffering was over. Samson went to prostitutes. Then he fell in love with a Philistine woman named Delilah and began having sexual relations with her without marrying her. God is long suffering and has plenty of mercy, but there does come a time when "enough is enough".

Delilah kept nagging Samson day after day asking him what the secret to his great strength was and how he could be tied up and subdued. "Hello Samson, get a clue! How stupid can you get and still breathe?" His story is just more proof that sin makes you dull and dimwitted! Delilah eventually wore Samson down and he told her everything. The devil is really great at wearing the saints down if they let him! That is why it is so important to nip his attacks in the bud! Samson told Delilah that no razor had ever been used on his head because he had been a Nazirite set apart to God since birth. If his head were shaved his strength would leave him and he would become as weak as any other man.

For Samson Did Not Know That the Lord Had Departed From Him

Judges 16:20 AMP
20 She said, The Philistines are upon you, Samson! And he awoke out of his sleep and said, I will go out as I have time after time and shake myself free. For Samson did not know that the Lord had departed from him.

What a sad commentary! Samson did not know that the Lord had departed from him! I cannot even imagine nor do I ever want to experience not knowing that the Lord has departed from me! This is why we need to remember that we are a spirit man having a physical experience. This is why we should not ever "play with the Anointing". What do I mean by that? Well if you have ever operated under a great Anointing, you can forget that you are limited to a physical body because under the Anointing you can feel like you can take on the world. It is as if you have stepped into another dimension. You are energized. But the fact remains that we are human. We have to take care of ourselves, spiritually, physically and mentally. God says, "It is not by might. It's not by power, but by My Holy Spirit"! We are only the gloves and God is the hand in the glove!

We must honor and esteem the Anointing! We must remember that without God there is no Anointing! Some people evidently think they can carry on adulterous relationships and other secret sins and still operate under the Anointing. The fact is they can, BUT only for a season. When that season is up there is hell to pay! Just like Samson, one day they will wake up not realizing that the Lord has departed from them. How insensitive, cold and far away from God would a person have to be to not know God had departed from them?

Galatians 3:3 AMP
3 Are you so foolish and so senseless and so silly?
Having begun [your new life spiritually] with the
[Holy] Spirit, are you now reaching perfection [by
dependence] on the flesh?

There are also those people who having begun in the Spirit they are now operating out of the flesh. They get off to a great start by daily staying plugged into the Holy Spirit. Little by little they allow fleshly distractions to pull them away from their spirit man and lose their bearings. I have heard it said if you are sailing a ship and get one degree off, it does not look like you are off course in the beginning, but the end result is being hundreds of miles from the intended destination.

Some people even cooperate with demonic activity, familiar spirits and such. Although the devil is not all knowing, he does know some things because we open our big mouths and tell him. That is why it is so important to *speak in unknown tongues—to be filled with the Holy Spirit—* because the devil cannot understand what we are saying to God. 1 Corinthians 14:2 reveal to us that when we speak in an unknown tongue we are not speaking to men, but to God. We are speaking secret truths, hidden things and mysteries. It is like a secret code and drives the devil crazy!

1 Corinthians 14:2 AMP
2 For one who speaks in an [unknown] tongue
speaks not to men but to God, for no one
understands or catches his meaning, because in
the [Holy] Spirit he utters secret truths and hidden
things [not obvious to the understanding].

1 Corinthians 14:2 KJV
2 For he that speaketh in an unknown tongue
speaketh not unto men, but unto God:
for no man understandeth him;
howbeit in the spirit he speaketh mysteries.

The word "mysteries" in the King James Version of 1 Corinthians 14:2 is translated:

musterion (moos-tay'-ree-on); from a derivative of muo (to shut the mouth); a secret or "mystery" (through the idea of silence imposed by initiation into religious rites): KJV - mystery.[1]

When we don't know what to pray, the Holy Spirit intercedes on behalf of us to God with yearnings and groaning too deep for utterance. These prayers are in accordance and in harmony with God's will [Romans 8:26-27]. You are praying the perfect prayer! You are praying God's will.

Romans 8:26-27 AMP
26 So too the [Holy] Spirit comes to our aid and
bears us up in our weakness; for we do not know
what prayer to offer nor how to offer it worthily
as we ought, but the Spirit Himself goes to meet
our supplication and pleads in our behalf with
unspeakable yearnings
and groanings too deep for utterance.
27 And He Who searches the hearts of men knows
what is in the mind of the [Holy] Spirit [what His
intent is], because the Spirit intercedes and pleads
[before God] in behalf of the saints <u>according to</u>
<u>and in harmony with God's will</u>. [Psalm 139:1,2.]

The Bible tells us that we build ourselves up when we pray in the Holy Spirit [Jude 20]. That is worth speaking in tongues all the time, on every occasion and in every season [Ephesians 6:18]!

Jude 20 AMP
20 But you, beloved, build yourselves up [founded]
on your most holy faith [make progress,
rise like an edifice higher and higher],
praying in the Holy Spirit;

Ephesians 6:18 AMP
18 Pray at all times (on every occasion, in every
season) in the Spirit, with all [manner of] prayer
and entreaty. To that end keep alert and watch with
strong purpose and perseverance, interceding in
behalf of all the saints (God's consecrated people).

How horrible it would be for you or I to say, "I will go out to minister under the Anointing as I have time after time" and not even know that the Lord had departed from us! It is a scary thing for any person to think they can live in habitual sin and be able to continue in God's sacred Anointing. God is merciful, but He is also just.

I just heard the Holy Spirit say, that as God's Presence and power increases, we are going to begin to see people who lie to the Holy Spirit fall dead just like Ananias and Sapphira did in Acts 5:1-11.

God is slow to anger and has plenty of mercy towards us and He is also longsuffering. Therefore, while people are in sin and growing apart from the intimacy with God, their spiritual senses get duller and duller. Suddenly they wake up not realizing God's manifested Presence has departed from them. Some people get too familiar with God, taking Him for granted. There is a difference between familiarity and the desired goal of intimacy with God.

We must remember to have a reverential fear of God. If we really love God with all our heart, soul, mind and strength, we will keep His commandments because we want to, not because we have to. It becomes our joy to please Him in every way possible...not get away with as much as possible!

By the time we see God's withdrawn manifested Presence from someone's life, God has given that person multiplied opportunities to repent. These things truly do not happen over night any more than a person who is pressing into God and pressing into God and pressing into God and faithfully serving God, seemingly is "all of a sudden" promoted by God. There was a lot of sitting at Jesus' feet, hard work, sweat and tears that took place first. If we are smart, there will be a lot of sitting at Jesus' feet, hard work, sweat and tears to stay there. Behind that suddenly was a lot of seemingly nothing...nothing...nothing...nothing and nothing.

Nobody just "oops I committed adultery"! There were the glances, thoughts, touches and actions that took place first. There was the ignoring of the Holy Spirit saying,

"Don't go there", until that person could not even hear The Holy Spirit's voice anymore. No one "suddenly" decides to embezzle thousands of dollars! Payday always comes good or bad. Like Eddie's Granny Edna Powell always told us, "God does not always pay on Friday, but He always pays." She's enjoying the ultimate payday in heaven with Jesus! True success is being obedient to God! So don't give up!

I Do Not Understand Why Ungodly People See People Saved, Healed, Filled With The Holy Spirit And Do Many Mighty Works In Jesus' Name!

How many times have you wondered why ungodly people see people saved, healed, filled with the Holy Spirit and do many mighty works in Jesus' name?

Matthew 7:20-23 AMP
20 Therefore, you will fully know
them by their <u>fruits.</u>
21 Not everyone who says to Me, Lord, Lord, will
enter the kingdom of heaven, but he who does the
will of My Father Who is in heaven.
22 Many will say to Me on that day, Lord, Lord,
have we not prophesied in Your name and driven
out demons in Your name and done many mighty
works in Your name?
23 And then I will say to them openly (publicly),
I never knew you; depart from Me, you who act
wickedly [disregarding My commands].

There were some men who would go to rural farming communities right after harvest time because they knew they could get a lot of money from the people. Their only purpose was to get the people's money. Yet under their ministry people would get saved, healed, and filled with the Holy Spirit.

During that time my husband's Great Uncle James Cain who had pioneered thirteen churches in Florida and is now in heaven with Jesus, was asked by group of Christian men, "How can these men who are charlatans, see people saved, healed, and even filled with the Holy Spirit when they are not even saved themselves?" Eddie's Uncle James answered, "If a married couple and an unmarried couple both practice the 'laws of reproduction' both could produce children. Having a child does not legitimatize the relationship."

Just because a man or woman may see many people healed, saved, and delivered in their meetings *does not mean God's validation is upon them at all.* Many people misread, Matthew 7:20 which says you will know a real man or woman of God by their fruit. They think "their fruit" means salvations, healings and so forth. The word "fruit" in Matthew 7:20 is the same word "fruit" in Galatians 5:22, [The Fruit of the Spirit] which is all about our Godly Character, not our works!

You can rest assured that as God's Word tells us in Galatians 6:7 we should not be deceived. God will not be mocked. Whatever a man sows he will reap. In other words "payday" comes for all us—good and bad! This is why it seems like many pastors and those in leadership seem to get away with hidden sin for such a long time and then God exposes them publicly.

Galatians 5:19-24 AMP
19 Now the doings (practices) of the flesh are clear
(obvious): they are immorality, impurity, indecency,
20 Idolatry, sorcery, enmity, strife, jealousy, anger
(ill temper), selfishness, divisions (dissensions),
party spirit (factions, sects with
peculiar opinions, heresies),
21 Envy, drunkenness, carousing, and the like.
I warn you beforehand, just as I did previously,

> *that those who do such things shall not inherit the*
> *kingdom of God.*
> *22 But the fruit of the [Holy] Spirit [the work*
> *which His presence within accomplishes] is love,*
> *joy (gladness), peace, patience (an even temper,*
> *forbearance), kindness, goodness*
> *(benevolence), faithfulness,*
> *23 Gentleness (meekness, humility), self-control*
> *(self-restraint, continence). Against such things*
> *there is no law [that can bring a charge].*
> *24 And those who belong to Christ Jesus (the*
> *Messiah) have crucified the flesh*
> *(the godless human nature) with its passions and*
> *appetites and desires.*

We need to know the difference between "charisma" and "Anointing". We need to know the difference between "hype" and "the Anointing". My husband had a distant cousin who I will call Zen to protect his name. Zen could take a church from 10 people to 200 plus people in a short period of time while all the time robbing the church blind, doing drugs, and living a very ungodly lifestyle. He could quote more Bible then most people have even read. [Note: The devil knows the Bible better than most of us] At one point Zen and his brother found out that an elderly couple at their dad's church kept cash money in their house instead of the bank. They slit the elderly lady's throat for money and she lived to identify them. Zen died in his fifties from the results of the drugs and ungodly living.

One day as Eddie and I were walking around the Sanford, Florida Flea Market, we met a man who asked Eddie if he was related to Zen. Of course, we were very reluctant to be associated with that cousin because we did not know if this would be one of his victims. The man told us, "I know Zen robbed our church blind, but I truly got saved and delivered from suicide for which I will always be grateful." He nicely reminded us that God's Word never returns to Him void [Isaiah. 55:11]! A donkey could present the Gospel of Jesus Christ [Numbers 22: 21-35] and people would get saved, healed, delivered and set free. The bottom line is that the Word of God is the Truth no matter what kind of vessel is presenting it. And The Word of God will produce a great harvest!

CHAPTER EIGHT

KEY #4 — OBEDIENCE

Unfortunately, King Saul along with all his other flaws had one great big flaw—DISOBEDIENCE! There is no such thing as partial obedience with God! A person either obeys or she/he rebels. With God there is nothing in-between.

God's Anointing Comes With Assignments
Saul is Anointed and Given an Assignment

1 Samuel 15:1-3 AMP
1 SAMUEL TOLD Saul, The Lord sent me to anoint you king over His people Israel. Now listen and heed the words of the Lord.
2 Thus says the Lord of hosts, I have considered and will punish what Amalek did to Israel, how he set himself against him in the way when [Israel] came out of Egypt.
3 Now go and smite Amalek and utterly <u>destroy all</u> they have; do not spare them, but kill both man and woman, infant and suckling, ox and sheep, camel and donkey.

You will see throughout the Bible that God's Anointing comes with assignments. God has you here on earth for a purpose. You have God-given assignments to complete. You have a God-given destiny to fulfill here on earth! Don't take King Saul's story too lightly, because we must remember that God has called us Kings and Priest unto Him. Basically, the more God gives us the more He requires of us. The greater the Anointing, the greater God's requirements of us!

Revelation 5:10 NKJV
10 And have made us kings and priests to our God;
And we shall reign on the earth."

Luke 12:48 AMP
48 But he who did not know and did things worthy
of a beating shall be beaten with few [lashes]. For
everyone to whom much is given, of him shall much
be required; and of him to whom men entrust much,
they will require and demand all the more.

King Saul's assignment was to utterly destroy ALL of Amalek and ALL they have – man, woman, infant, suckling, ox, sheep camel and donkey [1 Samuel 15:3]. I personally think these are very precise instructions. Last time I checked, the word "all" meant "all".

King Saul misused his Anointing and did not obey his God-given instructions and spared Agag, king of the Amalekites as well as the best of the sheep, oxen, fatlings, lambs and all that was good. In verse 11 of 1 Samuel, God told Samuel that he regretted making Saul king, because he had turned his back from following Him and did not perform His commands. God is not looking for robots or puppets, but He is looking for obedience!

In 1 Samuel 15:22-23 Samuel said to King Saul, "Has the Lord as great a delight in burnt offerings and sacrifices as in obeying the voice of the Lord? Behold, to obey is better than sacrifice, and to hearken than the fat of rams. For rebellion is as the sin of witchcraft, and stubbornness is as idolatry and teraphim (household good luck images). Because you have rejected the word of the Lord, He also has rejected you from being king."

It is no different when we disobey God. Not only does God look at disobedience as rebellion and stubbornness, God says that rebellion is as the sin of witchcraft and stubbornness is as idolatry and good luck images! In fact, disobedience is what got mankind thrown out of the Garden of Eden! The good news is that Jesus' obedience is what made us acceptable to God and brought us into right standing with God!

Romans 5:19 AMP
19 For just as by one man's disobedience (failing to hear, heedlessness, and carelessness) the many were constituted sinners, so by one Man's obedience the many will be constituted righteous (made acceptable to God, brought into right standing with Him).

Disobedience Caused Saul to Lose His Inheritance

1 Samuel 13:13-14 AMP
13 And Samuel said to Saul, You have done foolishly! You have not kept the commandment of the Lord your God, which He commanded you; for the Lord would have established your kingdom over Israel forever;
14 But now your kingdom shall not continue; the Lord has sought out [David] a man after His own heart, and the Lord has commanded him to be prince and ruler over His people, because you have not kept what the Lord commanded you.

King Saul's kingdom could have been established forever. However, the end result of King Saul's rebellion and disobedience to God was that God rejected King Saul from being King. He tore the Kingdom from Saul and gave it to David.

As stated before, the big difference between King Saul and King David was David took responsibility for his sin. He admitted that he not only sinned, but that his sin was against God. Then he asked for forgiveness! God sought out David because David had a heart after Him. King David's kingdom was established forever!

Oh, I want God to say, "I am seeking out Becky, a woman after My own heart"! How about you? Of course you will want to place your name and gender in place of mine.

The Anointing Manifests On The Day of Pentecost to the "Obedient Ones"

The manifested Presence of God or the Anointing came to the 120 obedient ones who were waiting in the Upper Room on the Day of Pentecost. They allowed the Holy Spirit to not only touch them, but to change them and to work through them to touch and change the world! This is the birth of the New Testament—New Covenant Church! And it remains God's blueprint for today's church!

Acts 1:4-5 NIV
4 On one occasion, while he was eating with
them, he gave them this command: "Do not leave
Jerusalem, but wait for the gift my Father promised,
which you have heard me speak about. 5 For John
baptized with water, but in a few days you will be
baptized with the Holy Spirit."

Acts 1:8 AMP
8 But you shall receive power (ability, efficiency,
and might) when the Holy Spirit has come upon
you, and you shall be My witnesses in Jerusalem
and all Judea and Samaria and to the ends (the very
bounds) of the earth.

After Jesus' resurrection from the dead, Jesus appeared to His followers over the next forty days [Acts 1:3] before ascending to the Father. In Acts 1:4-5, 8, Jesus shared His last words of instruction— a command, not an "if you feel like it" or "if it works out with your schedule".

Do not leave Jerusalem.
Wait for the gift [The Holy Spirit] my Father promised.

In a few days, the results of the disciple's obedience would be that:

You will be baptized in the Holy Spirit.
You will receive power [Ability, efficiency, and might
    are God's manifested Presence].
You will be My witnesses in Jerusalem and all Judea
    and Samaria and to the ends of the earth.

The Bible tells us when we receive the Anointing of the Holy Spirit; we receive *power, ability, efficiency and might!* We must keep in mind it is the Holy Spirit's power, ability, and efficiency and might working through us and with us; so we cannot nor should we take the credit for the operations of the Holy Spirit! It is a free gift so we cannot earn it. The 120 in the upper room only had to be *obedient* to follow Jesus' command!

When a person knows that they are about to die they do not waste their words being "chatty". Their last words are words they must feel to be enormously important to the hearers. If I knew I were about to die, I would make sure to communicate only the most crucial information to my loved ones—my last wishes, sentiments and instructions.

Jesus did not give his followers "the great suggestion". Jesus "commanded" his followers to go and wait in Jerusalem for the gift of the Holy Spirit, which His Father promised, and Whom Jesus spoke about. It was a "command" not the "great suggestion"!

We must remember something, the men and women who were waiting in the Upper Room for the "Holy Spirit" at Jesus' command in Acts 1:4-5, were people just like you and me. They did not know what or who the Holy Spirit was nor what He would look like. Would he look like Jesus? Would he be eight feet tall like the angels? How would they even know it was the Holy Spirit? Would He announce to them, "Hi, I'm the Holy Spirit"? And when the Holy Spirit did arrive, how could they be certain that it was He?

Having grown up in Pentecostal circles from the day I was born. I've often said that I cut my teeth on the church pews. Among other comparisons, I have heard the Holy Spirit compared to electricity, a dove, wind and oil. However, my point is that the Holy Spirit is not a dove. He is not oil, nor is He wind. He is not electricity. The Holy Spirit's attributes can be *compared to* the attributes or the characteristics of electricity, oil, fire [Acts 2:3], wind [John 3:8] or of a dove [Matthew 3:16]. The Holy Spirit is the third part of the Trinity! The Holy Spirit is a person, not a thing! The Holy Spirit is not tongues. He is a person distinct from the Father and the Son, though united to both in the oneness of the Godhead.

Matthew 28:19 AMP
19 Go then and make disciples of all the nations,
baptizing them into the name of the <u>Father</u> and of
the <u>Son</u> and of the <u>Holy Spirit</u>,

How would you like to be stuck in an upper room with a bunch of people for days, not knowing how many more days you would have to remain there to receive Jesus' promised gift of the Holy Spirit? Let's face it; John the Beloved had probably hugged the Apostle Peter one to many times for Peter's comfort level.

The Apostle Peter probably was praying much too loudly for some of them. They may have felt like telling Peter that God was not deaf.

Thomas was probably sitting around wringing his hands and "encouraging" others by saying, "I doubt that the gift of the Holy Spirit will ever come".

Did they leave to bathe? If not, I am sure that the aroma was not an enhancement to the whole drama. These people were real everyday people with feelings, preferences, points of views, and quirks just like you and me!

My dad, Ted Farina, who has now gone on to heaven to be with Jesus, was one of those people who prayed loudly. He and Peter would have gotten along quite well.

My mother, Geneva Farina, who has also gone on to heaven to be with Jesus, had a pet peeve. Whenever the person in charge asked everyone to join hands to pray, my mother said that holding hands was a great distraction to her and she wished people would quit asking the congregation to hold hands. I don't think she would have liked the Apostle John's touchy feely ways. She must have loved me a lot because as her pastor, I would occasionally ask everyone to join hands in prayer.

Joining hands in prayer never did and does not to this day bother me. The thing to remember is one is not right and the other wrong, they are just different—different strokes for different folks. Does this mean that we cannot be in agreement with other people whose ways of praying and touching God are different from our own? Clearly we can be in agreement with people whose personalities may even grate on our nerves. It happened on the Day of Pentecost. Our sole responsibility is to be "obedient" to God!

Let's take a look at the "Day of Pentecost"

Acts 2:1-4 NIV
1 When the day of Pentecost came, they were all together in one place. 2 Suddenly a sound like the blowing of a violent wind came from heaven and filled the whole house where they were sitting. 3 They saw what seemed to be tongues of fire that separated and came to rest on each of them. 4 All of them were filled with the Holy Spirit and began to speak in other tongues as the Spirit enabled them.

It is the tenth day since the 120 believers have entered the upper room to wait for the gift the Father promised as instructed by Jesus. All of the sudden, the sound of hurricane force winds enter the Upper Room. Tongues of fire came and rested upon each of them and they were ALL filled with the Holy Spirit with the Bible evidence of speaking in tongues.

Pastor Pandemonium

I heard about a Children's Pastor who was labeled "Pastor Pandemonium" who was doing a series on the Baptism of the Holy Spirit for the children and decided to reenact the Upper Room experience. He had rigged up a portable propane tank to his one side so all he would have to do is release the valve and allow the propane time to settle above his head. He also had an igniter in his other hand with a small pipeline that went up well above his head so that when he turned the igniter on it would cause the propane to ignite a flame above his head in the way of an illustrated sermon. The problem was that he allowed too much propane to release and unbeknown to him it settled in his hair and eyebrows and as he pressed the igniter—poof his hair and eyebrows were burnt off. It turns out that Pastor Pandemonium was okay other than the hair loss and some embarrassment. Although it probably did not seem funny at the time, you must admit that it causes quite a hilarious picture in your mind! Warning: Don't try this at home or church!!!

On the Day of Pentecost the Presence of God did manifest what appeared to be tongues of fire, which rested upon each one of the 120 people in the Upper Room as well as many other manifestations. Fire is symbolic of God's Presence [Exodus 19:18]. Hebrews 1: 7 and Psalms 104:4 tells us that God makes His ministers "flames of fire". This is the Birth of the New Testament—New Covenant Church! It remains God's blueprint for today's church!

The Tongue

James 1:26 NIV
*26 If anyone considers himself religious and yet
does not keep a tight rein on his tongue, he deceives
himself and his religion is worthless.*

James 3:5-6 AMP
*5 Even so the tongue is a little member, and it can
boast of great things. See how much wood or how
great a forest a tiny spark can set ablaze!
6 And the tongue is a fire. [The tongue is a] world of
wickedness set among our members, contaminating
and depraving the whole body and setting on fire*

the wheel of birth (the cycle of man's nature), being itself ignited by hell (Gehenna).

It is interesting to me that God takes the very thing we as human beings have the hardest time controlling, our tongue, and uses it to baptize us in the Holy Spirit. The best way to "tame our tongue" is to submit our tongue to the Holy Spirit and speak in tongues! If the tongue can do so much damage as James reports, how much more good can a tongue submitted to the Holy Spirit do?

Acts 2:5-21 tells us of the other "manifestations" that took place after the 120 were filled with the Holy Spirit as they began to leave the Upper Room.

Acts 2:5-21 NIV
5 Now there were staying in Jerusalem
God-fearing Jews from every nation under heaven.
6 When they heard this sound, a crowd came
together in bewilderment, because each one heard
them speaking in his own language. 7 Utterly
amazed, they asked: "Are not all these men who
are speaking Galileans? 8 Then how is it that
each of us hears them in his own native language?
9 Parthians, Medes and Elamites; residents of
Mesopotamia, Judea and Cappadocia, Pontus and
Asia, 10 Phrygia and Pamphylia, Egypt and the
parts of Libya near Cyrene; visitors from Rome
11(both Jews and converts to Judaism); Cretans and
Arabs-we hear them declaring the wonders of God
in our own tongues!" 12 Amazed and perplexed,
they asked one another, "What does this mean?"
13 Some, however, made fun of them and said,
"They have had too much wine."
14 Then Peter stood up with the Eleven, raised his
voice and addressed the crowd: "Fellow Jews and

*all of you who live in Jerusalem, let me explain this
to you; listen carefully to what I say. 15 These men
are not drunk, as you suppose. It's only nine in the
morning! 16 No, this is what was
spoken by the prophet Joel:
17 "'In the last days, God says,
I will pour out my Spirit on all people.
Your sons and daughters will prophesy,
your young men will see visions,
your old men will dream dreams.
18 Even on my servants, both men and women,
I will pour out my Spirit in those days,
and they will prophesy.
19 I will show wonders in the heaven above
and signs on the earth below,
blood and fire and billows of smoke.
20 The sun will be turned to darkness
and the moon to blood
before the coming of the great and
glorious day of the Lord.
21 And everyone who calls
on the name of the Lord will be saved.'*

Acts 2:38-41 NIV
*38 Peter replied, "Repent and be baptized, every
one of you, in the name of Jesus Christ for the
forgiveness of your sins. And you will receive the
gift of the Holy Spirit. 39 The promise is for you
and your children and for all who are far off-for all
whom the Lord our God will call."
40 With many other words he warned them; and
he pleaded with them, "Save yourselves from this
corrupt generation." 41 Those who accepted his
message were baptized, and about three thousand
were added to their number that day.*

The Results of the 120's Obedience
God's Manifested Presence or the Anointing

God's manifested Presence or the Anointing was the result of the 120's obedience. On the Day of Pentecost...suddenly a sound like the blowing of a violent wind came from heaven and filled the whole house where they were sitting with God's manifested Presence or the Anointing. *"Suddenly"* with God usually comes in the following manner...nothing, nothing, nothing, nothing, nothing, nothing, nothing, nothing, and then SUDDENLY.

God's manifested Presence or the Anointing was displayed in various ways on the Day of Pentecost:

* Tongues of fire.
* Speaking in other tongues.
* Outsiders heard some of the 120 Galileans declaring the wonders of God in their own non-Galilean languages.
* The 120 appeared to be drunk to some of the people. Peter told the people, "These men are not drunk, as you suppose. It's only nine in the morning! This is what was spoken by the prophet Joel".
* What do drunken people do?
    * They may not be able to walk a straight line.
    * They may dance about.
    * They laugh for no apparent reason.
    * They may slur their speech.
    * They may walk around saying, "I just love you man" and give you a great big hug and tell you how much God loves you!
    * They are less intimidated to say what's on their heart and mind. Bold!
    * They are generally more generous.

- They are less inhibited. Whatever is in them comes out. In this case they were saturated with the Holy Spirit of God so they were splashing God the Holy Spirit all over everyone!

The Apostle Peter was the very apostle who cursed and denied that he even knew Jesus three different times [John 18:17, 25, & 27] and went back to his old occupation of fisherman. Peter basically quit the ministry! And Peter did all this only fifty days prior to the Day of Pentecost. Now under the influence and saturation and baptism of the Holy Spirit Anointing, Peter is able to preach and leads about 3,000 people to Jesus and all 3,000 plus are baptized in water and in the Holy Spirit [Acts 2:38-41]! There were probably quite a few more than 3,000 people because when they counted people, they usually only counted the men with the exclusion of counting the women and children.

I sense as I sit here writing this passage that there are men and women in ministry who are about to quit or may have already quit. God is saying through me to you that it is not the time to quit! Get back up. Dust yourself off and do what He has told you to do! You are not a failure! God loves you! Everyone makes some mistakes, but that is not a license to quit. God can make a way where there seems to be no way. Ask Father God in the Name of Jesus to baptize you or to fill you once again, afresh with His precious Holy Spirit. He can do it again! He can restore every year that satan has stolen [Joel 2:25,26; Isaiah. 61:1-7]. Just like God did with Peter, God can transform you into a new woman or man with Holy Ghost boldness like you've never experienced before.

Any one of you, whether you are in ministry or not; if you will allow the Holy Spirit to fill, saturate and baptize you with Himself, will become a new bolder person and witness for the cause of Christ!

I want to share a *hot off the press modern day testimony* of God using someone to communicate to another person through speaking in tongues. One of my dear friends, Pastor Hope MacDonald and her husband, Pastor Ed MacDonald went on a mission trip to Chincah, Peru this past summer. Hope had been under a great physical attack right before going on the trip to Peru and questioned if she should even go. After purposing in her heart to go, Hope received a miracle—the spots on her lungs were gone! Praise God Hope did not let the devil stop her from being obedient and fulfilling her God-given assignment! Here is the email account of her amazing experience below.

Hi Becky,

We are back. What an awesome, exciting, powerful in the Spirit, anointed, loving, caring, etc. time. Thanks for praying for us.

The Peruvian People are wonderful and so open to the gospel. We had such an Anointing and mighty things were accomplished in the Name of our wonderful Savior and Lord. There is one experience I must share that has never happened to me before.

We went to the Training University that we helped start that are training men and women for the ministry located in Chincah, Peru. The oldest daughter, Maria Isabel is already a minister in a church. It was her father's church and he is in charge of the school.

Well we were ministering around the altar and people were so open to receive so much, much was done. Maria Isabella was in the aisle of the church looking very sober. I did not speak any Spanish (I'm learning a little now) but felt strongly that I needed to hold her and pray for her to receive whatever she needed. I knew God had ministered to her, but I didn't know the extent. After almost everyone else had left

she came up to our missionary friend and asked for him to interpret for me. She told me that God had been recently giving her direction but she wasn't sure whether it was what she should really do. Anyway, God changed my tongue and I spoke fluent Spanish and told her all about the situation and the direction she was to go. She was so thankful that I had come and <u>been obedient</u> (emphasis mine) to the Lord. Isn't that awesome? I have heard of this happening before but never had experience it.
Love ya,
Hope

If God can use Hope and God is absolutely no respecter of persons [Acts 10:34], then maybe today it will be your privilege and honor to be used by the Holy Spirit in this manner! We are not waiting on God. He is waiting on us! Don't say, "God will never use me". Instead say, "God, here am I, use me!" Then be obedient! Most of the time God asks us to do things we do not feel capable of doing so He gets all the glory!

Philippians 4:13 AMP
13 I have strength for all things in Christ Who empowers me [I am ready for anything and equal to anything through Him Who infuses inner strength into me; I am self-sufficient in Christ's sufficiency].

Heaven or Hell?

1 Corinthians 15:3-4 AMP
3 For I passed on to you first of all what I also had received, that Christ (the Messiah, the Anointed one) died for our sins in accordance with [what] the Scriptures [foretold], [Isaiah 53:5-12.]

4 That He was buried, that He arose on the third day as the Scriptures foretold, [Psalms 16:9,10.]

Maybe you've never accepted Jesus Christ as your Lord and Savior before. Here is a good litmus test. Do you know that God loves you and has a great plan for your life? Do you know if you were to die in the next five minutes where you would spend eternity—heaven or hell? There is a real heaven to gain and a real hell to shun! Are you one hundred percent sure that if you died in the next five minutes that you would spend eternity in heaven with Jesus? Your answer cannot be anything but that you are one hundred percent sure that if you died in the next five minutes, you know beyond any shadow of a doubt, that you would spend eternity in heaven, because you have asked Jesus to forgive you of your sin and accepted Him as your only Lord and Savior. If you could not answer, "Yes I am one hundred percent, absolutely sure that I am going to heaven when I die." then I want you to *pray this prayer out loud*:

Heavenly Father,

I admit that I am not sure if I were to die in the next five minutes that I would go to heaven to live with you for eternity.

I believe that Jesus Christ is the only Son of God—Your only Son, Father God.

I believe that Jesus Christ died on the cross for my sin, according to the scriptures.

I believe that Jesus Christ rose from the dead on the third day and that He is now seated next to You in heaven ever interceding for me.

I acknowledge I am a sinner and ask You to forgive me of my sin.

I receive Jesus Christ into my heart as my Lord and Savior. Thank you for forgiving me. Jesus, thank you for dying on the cross for me!

I decree that if I were to die anytime in the future that I am forgiven and I am going to heaven to live with you forever.

I confess that You, Father God have God-given assignments for me here on earth. I choose to fulfill my assignments.

I have a destiny in You, Father God. I am not going to heaven one day before you are ready for me to come! I choose life!

I choose the Anointing—Your manifested Presence. God, here I am, use me!

In the Name of Jesus,
Amen

Now that you have received Jesus Christ as your Lord and Savior I tell you as a minister of the Gospel that you are saved. You are forgiven. You are going to heaven when you die and you have God-given assignments to complete here on earth. You are not an accident. You are here by divine destiny and by divine design! Now it is time for you to ask to be filled with the Holy Spirit just like the 120 were on the Day of Pentecost and just like people all over the world are being filled with the Holy Spirit today.

Before you pray the following prayer, I want you to read the next scripture out loud:

Luke 11:11-13 AMP
11 What father among you, if his son asks for a loaf of bread, will give him a stone; or if he asks for a fish, will instead of a fish give him a serpent?
12 Or if he asks for an egg, will give him a scorpion?

13 If you then, evil as you are, know how to give good gifts [gifts that are to their advantage] to your children, <u>how much more will your heavenly Father give the Holy Spirit to those who ask and continue to ask Him!</u> [Emphasis Mine]

As you pray this prayer, you now know that if you ask God to baptize you with the Holy Spirit that is exactly what you are going to receive. Pray this prayer out loud and begin to speak in tongues as the Holy Spirit gives you clear loud expression:

Heavenly Father,

I come to you in the Name of Jesus. I ask you to baptize me, saturate me, and fill me with the Holy Spirit, so that the same Holy Spirit Anointing to touch and change the world that came upon the 120 people in the Upper Room according to Acts 2 may touch and change me too. I receive by faith the Holy Spirit infilling as the Holy Spirit comes upon me and gives me utterance. I choose to allow the Anointing power—Your ability, efficiency and might—to not only come upon me, but to come in me to change me. To manifest through me to touch and change the world! I decree that I will never be the same again. I decree that I have received and will operate in the Anointing to be Jesus' witness at home and abroad. I decree that I will <u>continually be being filled</u> with the Holy Spirit so that I can continually be touching heaven and changing earth! Thank you Holy Spirit for baptizing me in You! I submit my tongue to You right now, Holy Spirit.

In the Name of Jesus,
Amen

Just receive! This is not the time to pray. You've already done that. Now do not speak in any languages you already know and just receive and begin to speak in the new language the Holy Spirit gives you no matter how strange it may feel or sound. Remember if you ask The Father to fill you with the Holy Spirit, then what happens? You are filled with the Holy Spirit!

Please contact me if you prayed either or both of these prayers at www.BeckyFarinaCain.com

I encourage each of you who have prayed either or both of the prayers above to go and tell someone what just happened to you.

The results of Disobedience
(380 People MIA—Missing In Action)

The 120 people [Acts 1:12-14] in the Upper Room, consisted of Peter, John, James, Andrew, Philip, Thomas, Bartholomew, Matthew; James son of Alphaeus, Simon the Zealot, and Judas [son] of James, with the women and Mary the mother of Jesus, and with His brothers. They had been in the Upper Room for 10 days when the Holy Spirit baptized (or saturated and soaked) them. Where were the rest of the over five hundred other people Jesus showed Himself to after His resurrection according to 1 Corinthians 15:6? There were at least 380 people who missed out on the outpouring on The Day of Pentecost!

Matthew 10:38 AMP
38 And he who does not take up his cross and follow
Me [cleave steadfastly to Me, conforming wholly to
My example in living and, if need be, in dying also]
is not worthy of Me

There is a BIG difference between someone who **says** they are a "follower of Christ" and a person whose life exemplifies that they are a true "follower of Christ"! Like I've heard it said, "You can say you are a car. You can even go and sit in the garage and say you are a car, but that does not make you a car". It is not so much what you "say", but it is what you "do"—your obedience! It is who you are.

Many people miss their touch from God through His Holy Spirit, because they are after a "microwave" experience that may require "crock pot" tenacity! Maybe they allowed the "cares of this world" to rob them of this glorious outpouring. It appears to me that the other 380 plus people—"followers", did not have the same resolve as the 120 "true followers" of Christ had and they truly missed out! The 380 may have just been downright disobedient, or rebellious to follow the command to *"Do not leave Jerusalem, but wait for the gift my Father promised, which you have heard me speak about"*.

We are talking about 380 people who saw Jesus after His resurrection and who witnessed Jesus ascending up into heaven in a cloud! What more would it have taken to move these people? Matthew 10:38 tell us that the 380 people were not worthy of Jesus! How would you liked to have been the person who just left minutes before the outpouring of the Holy Ghost to go home and take a break instead of adhering to Jesus' command to stay in the Upper Room until the gift of Holy Spirit was given?

We must be ready to give our lives even unto the death if that is what is required of us! I think that we have been handed a "watered down gospel"! We are not going to get to heaven by joining a church and going up to shake the preachers hand! Being a follower of Christ requires a lifetime of obedience and commitment! I have to tell you that even in my darkest hour I would rather be a follower of Christ than the seemingly "wealthiest" woman in the world! And I am not saying that God is against us having wealth. He's against wealth having us. What I am saying is what a Psalm of the sons of Korah said:

Psalms 84:10 AMP
10 For a day in Your courts is better than a
thousand [anywhere else]; I would rather be a
doorkeeper and stand at the threshold in the house
of my God than to dwell [at ease]
in the tents of wickedness.

Modern Day Example of Missing God Through Disobedience

God anointed and appointed me to write this book. I had to accept the appointment and the Anointing to write this book and then I had to do it –faith without works is dead! I have heard several testimonies where people said that God told them that they were not God's first choice. As far as I know, I am God's first choice to write "7 Keys to the Anointing".

I was in my kitchen cooking one day and I had the television on in the family room. I could hear the speaker speaking and I don't know what Christian channel was on or who the speaker was. In an effort to cause the least amount of confusion in relaying what I heard, I will refer to:

- The speaker as Joe
- The Pastor as Pastor Rejoice
- The church as First Church of the Happy Saints.

Joe said that he had recently spoken with Pastor Rejoice and Pastor Rejoice said he was God's 7th choice to be the pastor of First Church of the Happy Saints. When God called Pastor Rejoice to start the

First Church of the Happy Saints, he was very hesi-
tant. God told Pastor Rejoice, "You are my 7th choice.
I've already been turned down six times." So Pastor
Rejoice decided to step up to the plate and obey God
and now he has a very thriving church where people
are getting saved weekly.

There was a well-dressed man who looked like
a prosperous businessman who kept coming to the
First Church of the Happy Saints, but every time the
altar call was given he sat there and looked tormented
and then would promptly leave. "Did he need to get
saved?", Pastor Rejoice wondered. Why did this man
who seemingly was distraught at coming to First
Church of the Happy Saints continue coming?

This went on for six months until one day this
wealthy, yet distraught man made an appointment to
meet with Pastor Rejoice. When the man walked into
Pastor Rejoices' office, he handed Pastor Rejoice a set
of old blueprints. When Pastor Rejoice looked at the
blueprints, he realized that they were an exact dupli-
cate of First Church of the Happy Saints' building
only these blueprints were made years before First
Church of the Happy Saints began.

Then the man began to tell Pastor Rejoice, "I
was God's first choice to start First Church of the
Happy Saints. As you can see God even gave me the
blueprints of the building years before you obeyed
Him. Every week when I see all of the people getting
saved, I can't help but think that those people would
not have gotten the opportunity to receive Jesus if
you had not obeyed Him and started First Church of
the Happy Saints! I regret that I began to obey God
in starting First Church of the Happy Saints, but did
not see it through. I wanted to tell you thank you for
being obedient!"

I don't know about you, but I don't want to be a person who doesn't do what God has asked me to do and live to see another person fulfill my assignment! There are those times when what you were assigned to do will never get accomplished unless you do it, but there are other times when God will keep on going to one person after another until one of them picks up her or his cross and follows Jesus!

I Am A Product Of Someone's Obedience

I am a product of an obedient Holy Spirit filled woman! When we were pastors in Deltona, Florida, we were meeting in the "cafetorium" of an elementary school. A "cafetorium" is an auditorium that doubles as the schools cafeteria. I believe the year was 1998. To my surprise a couple who I had not seen since I was thirteen years old, named Jake and Antoinette Scalfri came to our church in the cafetorium. People used to call their son Larry and me "kissing cousins". Antoinette, whose nickname was Toni, asked if she could share a testimony with the congregation. I am so glad she did since she has gone on to be with Jesus and I would never have known how my dad's family came to know Jesus. To the best of my recollection, Toni said that her Italian grandmother was living in Milwaukee, Wisconsin during the depression. The Farina family lived in Racine, Wisconsin. Toni told how that her grandmother had been praying in tongues at home and God spoke to her to go to Racine, Wisconsin, to the family Farina at such and such street and to tell them about Jesus. She had quite a predicament. Since this was during the Great Depression, she did not have a car and it was a thirty-three mile trip. Most people did not own a car. But Toni's grandmother's son-in-law did have a car. The son-in-law was gracious enough to agree to drive her to Racine. It is important to understand that Toni's grandmother did not even know in the natural if there was a family called Farina. She had to step out totally on faith. The trip was costly due to the depression. What if she missed God? She absolutely heard God and went to the home of the family called Farina and led them to the Lord. My grandson, Peyton Cain is the fifth generation of the family called Farina that knows about Jesus because a sweet Holy Spirit filled, on fire, praying grandmother, listened to and obeyed the Holy Spirit's leading!

May we all willingly and with a happy heart fulfill every assignment God has for us to fulfill here on earth! If we are honest with ourselves, His cross is a much better cross to bear than the cross of disobedience! Who knows how many generations of lives God will use us to touch. All these years later, Toni's grandmother's obedience is still touching and changing lives today.

CHAPTER NINE

KEY # 5—TAKE GOOD CARE OF YOURSELF, YOU BELONG TO GOD!

We must guard the Anointing by getting enough rest and taking care of our body, which is called "The Temple of the Holy Spirit". While it is true that "one touch can change your life", it is equally true that we must continually be being filled with the Holy Spirit to flow in the Anointing. We all leak!

1 Corinthians 6:19-20 AMP
19 Do you not know that your body is the temple
(the very sanctuary) of the Holy Spirit Who lives
within you, Whom you have received [as a Gift]
from God? You are not your own, 20 You were
bought with a price [purchased with a preciousness
and paid for, made His own]. So then, honor God
and bring glory to Him in your body

I am a living testament of what can happen if you do not continually abide in His Presence and take care of yourself. During the great revivals, we were experiencing people getting saved, healed spiritually, physically, mentally, and financially. I can't tell you the numbers of people who were delivered from suicide and depression in the meetings we conducted. Then to my surprise, I found myself suicidal. If you had asked me, I would have told you that I was just fine and that I was just feeling a little down because that is what I believed.

What had happened is many times the love offering the churches gave us was what some in Christian circles unfortunately call, "a lot of love and no offering". Of course if there had been a lot of love, there would have been a lot of offering. We would minister in churches where it got back to us that the church did not give us the entire offering. Basically, not only did they steal from our family, but also they stole from the Lord!

Before we followed God's leading to go on the road as evangelist, we were co-pastoring a church with a nice salary—a regular income that we could plan on and budget. Hindsight is 20-20, but in the midst of the financial storm I began listening to satan say, "You are going to lose your home." I would think over and over again, "Oh, we are going to lose our home". Then satan would say, "You are going to lose your car". I began rehearsing what satan was saying to me. Now remember, I would have told you that I was just a little down. I did not realize that I was suicidal. I would pray things like, "God please just take me home now. Jennifer and Eric are old enough for Eddie to take care of alone and I don't want to be here anymore."

Before you start polishing your halo, I am not the first, nor will I be the last person to experience being suicidal. Let's take a look at the Great Prophet Elijah as an example. One minute Elijah is on Mount Carmel [1 Kings 18] making a mockery out of 450 Prophets of Baal by himself. Although Elijah was a great prophet, he was still a man just like you and me. Therefore, in the natural there is absolutely no way Elijah could have killed 450 men all by himself! Elijah had to have "supernatural strength in order to accomplish such a feat!

Then Elijah tells King Ahab to go home because the three and one half year drought is about to end. It is going to rain! It not only rained, but it was a major down pouring of pelting rain. Elijah proceeds to outrun King Ahab and his chariots to get to safety by running twenty miles on foot. How could Elijah do this? Obviously, Elijah could not do it in his natural strength and ability. Elijah did these "signs and wonders" under the Anointing. One man cannot kill 450 men by himself. A man cannot cause it to rain after a 3-½ year drought. In the natural, a man cannot outrun a chariot and horses for 20 miles. Especially when the King had the best and swiftest horses in the land! Elijah was not operating in the natural, but under the Anointing. Remember "the Anointing", is God's ability, efficiency and might that come upon an individual. The Anointing is God's manifested Presence and power.

After operating in such a great Anointing and witnessing these things himself, you would think that Elijah would never have another day of doubt or fear and would forever trust God with his very being. Not so! All it took to shake Elijah out of the Anointing and into fear and doubt, was Queen Jezebel's threatening to kill Elijah like Elijah killed her prophets of Baal.

How did I finally realize that I was suicidal? One evening my husband came home, went into our bedroom, and turned on the television. Suddenly I heard Bishop T.D. Jakes on television and went into our bedroom to fuss at Eddie for not telling me Bishop Jakes was on. After all, Eddie knows how much I love hearing Bishop Jakes preach…. he's a preaching machine! When I got into the bedroom I realized that Eddie was asleep. It is beyond me how anyone can sleep through

Bishop Jakes. As I am writing this God reminded me that He was orchestrating my deliverance. That is why Eddie was asleep.

Just as I entered the room, Bishop Jakes said something like, "There are people being set free from the spirit of suicide right now. Spirit of suicide, I command you to let them go right now in Jesus name!" As soon as he said that, I could not see the television, Eddie, or our bedroom anymore. I was in complete darkness—zero light! The next thing I see is a door opening with a beautiful light emanating from the other side of the door. An angel walked in and escorted me out of the complete darkness and into His marvelous light and he seated me in this huge adult size golden beanbag like chair—very cushy—where about six angels began to minister to me. Instantly I was made aware that I had had a spirit of suicide and was now completely free! Whenever I feel the darkness I sensed back in that room moving in on me now—which is not very often, I say out loud, "I will not go back in that darkness. I have closed that door!"

By the way, we never lost anything. Both of our children received one hundred percent scholarships to any Florida college of their choosing including money for books! Not only that, but some years later after my mom's home going to see Jesus, we sold our home for a good profit and bought my parents home which sits on three quarters of an acre—an upgrade from our previous home. Before we knew it, we owned both of our vehicles debt free! The devil is a liar. We serve a faithful God!

1 Kings 19:1-4 AMP
1 AHAB TOLD Jezebel all that Elijah had done and
how he had slain all the prophets
[of Baal] with the sword.
2 Then Jezebel sent a messenger to Elijah, saying,
So let the gods do to me, and more also, if I make

> *not your life as the life of one of them*
> *by this time tomorrow.*
> *3 Then he was afraid and arose and went for his life*
> *and came to Beersheba of Judah [over eighty miles,*
> *and out of Jezebel's realm] and left*
> *his servant there.*
> *4 But he himself went a day's journey into the*
> *wilderness and came and sat down under a lone*
> *broom or juniper tree and asked that he might die.*
> *He said, It is enough; now, O <u>Lord, take away my*
> *life</u>; for I am no better than my fathers.*

As you can see in 1 Kings 19:4, Elijah wanted to end his life. Sound familiar? What we are not aware of is how physically and mentally tired Elijah probably had gotten. Once the Anointing lifts, we have the natural to deal with! I have often thought about the fact that even though Elijah was operating under the Anointing, he was a human being with a nature like we have and just plain got tired—perhaps even exhausted. We need to take care of our bodies and minds by getting plenty of good rest and nutrition!

> *James 5:17 AMP*
> *17 <u>Elijah was a human being with a nature such*
> *as we have</u> [with feelings, affections, and a*
> *constitution like ours]; and he prayed earnestly for*
> *it not to rain, and no rain fell on the earth for three*
> *years and six months.*

All too often the "man or woman of God" begins to think they are invincible and impervious to the attacks of the enemy. After all satan's whole mission is to steal from us, kill us and destroy us. Let each of us take thought lest we too find ourselves after leaving a heavily anointed service or series of heavily anointed services so exhausted that we give the enemy of our souls a foothold. Before we know it, we too want to end it all. We must get proper rest for our bodies and minds! We cannot do proper warfare when we are exhausted! We cannot make good decisions when we are exhausted. It is easier not to recognize the lies of the enemy when we are tired. It is easier to listen to the lies of the enemy when we are worn out!

God specifically tells us that we are to take a Sabbath Rest—one day out of seven. Even in the beginning of creation, God created for six days and on the seventh day He rested. *If God had to take a day of rest, how much more do you and I need to take one day out of seven days to rest!* Do we really think that we know better than our Creator? God is not in as big of a hurry as we are. There are hungry people out there waiting to be told the True Gospel through vessels of honor who are totally surrendered to the Father! As we take up our crosses to follow Him, may we take the time to rest!

Matthew 10:38 AMP
And he who does not take up his cross and follow
Me [cleave steadfastly to Me, conforming wholly to
My example in living and, if need be, in dying also]
is not worthy of Me.

If Jesus had to be anointed by God, then how much more do we need God to anoint us [Acts 10:38]? If Jesus had to take time out to go and pray and be in God's Presence in order to minister to the people, how much more do we need to draw away for a season of refreshing from God? You cannot give what you do not have! We must recognize that Jesus is the Anointer. We are the anointed! Without Him we are nothing!

There was a period of time in my life where I kept hearing an old song—jingle from some television commercial. In fact, it is the Holy Spirit Who just brought it back to my remembrance. The words were *"Take good care of yourself, you belong to me"*. Frankly, I cannot even remember what it was advertising. Yet, I finally realized that it was God singing to me and trying to get me to start taking better care of myself. I believe that God wants all of us to take good care of ourselves, because we do belong to Him! I am still a work in progress and so are you.

CHAPTER TEN

KEY #6—ARE YOU HUNGRY?

Matthew 5:6 AMP
6 Blessed and fortunate and happy and spiritually
prosperous (in that state in which the born-again
child of God enjoys His favor and salvation) are
those who <u>hunger and thirst</u> for righteousness
(uprightness and right standing with God), for they
shall be completely satisfied! [Isaiah 55:1,2.]

John 7:37-39 AMP
37 Now on the final and most important day of the
Feast, Jesus stood, and He cried in a loud voice, If
any man is <u>thirsty</u>, let him come to Me and drink!
38 He who believes in Me [who cleaves to and
trusts in and relies on Me] as the Scripture has said,
From his innermost being shall flow <u>[continuously]</u>
springs and rivers of living water.
39 But He was speaking here of the Spirit, Whom
those who believed (trusted, had faith) in Him were
afterward to receive. For the [Holy] Spirit had not
yet been given, because Jesus was not yet glorified
(raised to honor). [Emphasis Mine]

You must be hungry and thirsty for the things of God! Until you get so hungry and so thirsty for God to touch you that nothing else matters, you won't experience the total Anointing/infilling of the Holy Spirit in and upon or through your life! How bad do you want the touch of God on your life? You must get desperate! You must get hungry! You must be parched with a thirst that can only be quenched by God Himself! The great news is when we hunger and thirst for the things of God, He promises us that we will be filled! So get ready! The best is yet to come!

We've already discussed the Anointing looking like hurricane force winds in a room, tongues of fire appearing above the heads of the 120 believers in the Upper room; people speaking in unknown tongues declaring the wonders of God in the native tongues of the people listening and people staggering around like drunks. Well wonders are still happening today to those who are hungry for more of God and His Presence!

It happened one summer in the early 1990's; during a Vacation Bible School at the church my husband Eddie and I were co-pastoring in Florida. We were renting a 5,000 or so square foot storefront building. It had very little outside play area. As part of the Vacation Bible School program, we planned for each age group to have a short time outdoors with our limited space.

Unfortunately, the air conditioning units were in the play area and one of the air conditioning units had an exposed wire unbeknown to us. As Florida weather goes, it rained almost every day and the ground by the air conditioners was wet. When you add an exposed electrical wire, water and a rambunctious three-year-old boy, you have a recipe for disaster! The small boy saw the exposed wire, which none of the rest of us saw and touched it! As he lay curled up in a fetal position, his hands had to be loosed from the connection. He was rushed to the emergency room. It was confirmed that the electricity had made a complete circuit in his body. Praise God, the young child was miraculously protected by God and suffered no ill effects from the experience!

The Holy Spirit can be "compared to" the *attributes* or the *characteristics* of a dove, oil, wind or electricity. If you were to go and stick your finger in an electrical socket, you would definitely have a physical reaction just as the 3 year old had. You may not fall down into a fetal position, but you will have a definite reaction! The same is true if you plug into the Holy Spirit, so to speak. You will have a definite reaction! I am not suggesting that you go and stick your finger in an electrical socket to find out. I'm sure it could be a hair-raising experience! But I am recommending that you plug into the Holy Spirit! You will truly never be the same again!

Now think about it, you cannot actually physically "see" electricity, but you can absolutely "SEE" the results of the electricity! You can absolutely "FEEL" the results of the electricity! You can absolutely "EXPERIENCE" in a "TANGIBLE" way the electricity and that "experience of the tangible" electricity can have a permanent and powerful effect upon you! The same can be said of the Anointing. The Anointing cannot physically be "seen" in the natural, but when the "Anointing of the Holy Spirit" touches your life, you can absolutely "SEE" the results of the Anointing. Just as different people will act, sound, and feel differently when they put their finger in an electrical outlet, different people will act, sound, and feel differently when the "The Anointing" touches them. Same power. Different reaction.

Your reaction to the Anointing and another person's reaction to the Anointing may be and probably will be different. One thing is for certain; you will have a reaction! You may feel something like goose bumps. Some people feel heat come over their body. Others seem to get frozen in place. You will have a tangible experience that can be seen, heard and felt! You will "feel" the Holy Spirit Anointing in and on your physical body! The Anointing is tangible! You can absolutely "EXPERIENCE" in a "TANGIBLE" way the "Anointing" of the Holy Spirit and that "experience of the tangible 'Anointing'" can have a permanent effect upon you and others around you *if* you allow it to!

Are there people who get in the flesh when the Holy Spirit manifests His Presence? Absolutely. Should we not press in for the manifested Presence of God because of these zealots? Absolutely not! You and I should never allow the fleshly zealots to stop us from being hungry and pursuing the real touch of God! Two of my brother-in-laws went to a Christian University [I am omitting the name of the college because it in no way reflects upon the college itself]. A person sincerely getting in the flesh happens everywhere. The incident took place in the college chapel. During chapel time a young man got up and said, "God just told me to run through that wall." After making that statement, the young man proceeded to "run through the wall". Of course he just hit the wall going full steam and was knocked to the floor. The funniest part of this story is that the young man then said as he was lying on the floor, "God just told me never do that again!"

I want to add a comment to the pastors and leaders reading this right now. It truly is better to have a little wild fire than it is to quench the Presence of God. God has a way of dealing with the wild fire as he did with the zealous college student. You yourself can handle a few zealots. Do not rob yourself, your followers or God of a true move of God's manifested Presence. Revivals, renewals, outpourings—whatever you call them—can be messy. Changing diapers is messy and raising children is work! Should we stop procreating because it's just too much trouble? No!

My husband and I actually had a pastor tell us one time during the days of the Brownsville Revival in Pensacola, Florida where I've heard that over 100,000 people got saved and over one million people came through the doors, that he did not want to have a "Brownsville Revival" because it required too much work. He was happy with his large congregation, nice paycheck and so forth. He did not want to rock the boat. I have a serious question to ask each and every leader, "Are you in leadership to do God's will, your will, or man's will"? Jesus said in Hebrews 10:7, "I have come to do Your will Oh God."

My husband and I were attending Calvary Assembly of God in the 1970's into the early 1980's before any one of us had ever heard of Benny Hinn. Then Benny began dating Suzanne, the daughter of Senior Pastor Roy and Pauline Harthern. As a result, Benny Hinn did a few services at Calvary Assembly in Winter Park, Florida.

Eddie and I were in the choir—newlyweds ourselves at the time and as much as I enjoyed the "feeling" of the Presence of God or the "Anointing", I was not too keen on the manifestations. Specifically the "being slain in the Spirit", as they called it back then. I did not mind seeing others fall under God's powerful Anointing, but I was not too thrilled at the prospect of being the recipient of such a touch of God. Frankly it scared me. I would stand in the choir trying to make sure my knees were locked so I would not succumb to falling in the Spirit. I managed to succeed, but little did I realize I would later become one of the biggest Holy Ghost lushes in the Spirit. To this day I still can never get enough of God's Presence touching my life!!! It wasn't long after the meetings at Calvary Assembly of God that I was working at WAJL (Where We Acclaim Jesus Lord) Radio station as a Traffic Controller.

Benny Hinn came in to record his radio broadcast. When he walked past my desk, to my great surprise, I felt a huge swoosh of the Holy Spirit! A GREAT HUNGER for God's Presence came upon me and has never left me. From that moment on I was determined to walk in that same Holy Spirit Anointing! I am not talking about a healing Anointing, although I do walk in God's healing Anointing. I am talking about walking with the Holy Spirit in such a way that His Presence is overflowing all around me making others hungry for Him! Give me His Presence over everything else. Let me be so in love with Him that the people around me get hungry and thirsty for Him!!!

Just a little side note—Benny Hinn was the first person to publicly proclaim that there was a call to ministry on both Eddie's and my lives. I don't know if Benny Hinn is even aware of how God has used him in our lives. This particular Sunday night in 1985 or 1986, my husband said, "I don't know why because we have never attended one of Benny Hinn's church services before, but I feel it is imperative that we attend tonight." We were attending another local church and had always been of the mind-set that we would be loyal to our church by not attending another church. As noble as that sounds, our church did not even have Sunday evening services and God did not have a problem with our visiting another part of His Body. God even worked out a babysitter for our two children. Some of our mind-sets are just religious boxes and ideas. We need to let God out of the box and then let go of the box!

Eddie and I, along with my sister Terri and her husband Paul went to Orlando Worship Center (Benny Hinn's church) that Sunday night. The only problem was we were unaware that it was a special Sunday evening healing service. We wondered why we needed to be at a healing service. Well at one point, Benny Hinn said God is healing people from sinus conditions and you will probably feel a heat or warmth on your sinus area. I felt a heat come upon my sinus passages and I could breath freer. Then Benny said, if you don't come to the front you would lose your healing. Ugh! We were all the way up in the balcony and I preferred to remain anonymous. Then when he said it again, I decided that I did not want to lose my healing so I proceeded going down stairs to the bottom floor. Suddenly I realized that Eddie was standing near me. When we discussed the evening later on, he said that he was not going to let me get something and him get nothing.

God does know how to move us! We were standing in this long line of people as Benny Hinn began coming down the line praying for people. By the way, I no longer had a problem with going out in the Spirit anymore. When Benny got to Eddie and me, Benny made some kind of noise like "Whoa" and said, "Don't let that couple go." Therefore, when we got up off the floor, we were escorted to the platform. Benny said, "These two have a great call to the ministry on them". The interesting part of this is that Eddie and I had not told anyone but each other that we felt like God was calling us into the ministry.

God used Benny Hinn to confirm His call upon our lives. After having a little fun with us—Benny must have had them pick us up and he prayed over us at least three times. We ended up in the bushes on the platform and they left us there. Then the service was over. When we were finally able to pick ourselves up off the floor, my legs felt like spaghetti noodles and so did Eddie's. We managed to get off the platform. Then I looked at ALL those stairs up to the balcony. There might as well have been 1,000 stairs. I knew my legs were not cooperating! Thankfully, my sister Terri and her husband Paul saw that we were having problems. They gathered our belongings and brought them down to us. I did not know it then, but Eddie and I were what is called "being drunk in the Holy Spirit". Being "drunk in the Holy Spirit" is another manifestation of the Anointing. Suffice it to say it is wonderful!

Well no one can call Benny Hinn a false prophet to me. At the time he prayed for us we were leading a Young Adults group as volunteers. In 1987 we were hired on at a church as the Youth Pastors. In 1988, we pioneered our first church. To this day we have served God with all our heart, soul, mind and strength!

It is also interesting to note that Benny acknowledged the call on the lives of both Eddie and me. We are both ordained ministers. We have been co-pastors, co-evangelists and as Eddie so humorously says, "We are Co-Cain's". My daughter, Jen Patterson calls us the "Dynamic Duo". If you need a scriptural reference for this, God used the husband and wife team of Priscilla and Aquila [See Acts Chapter 18]. Eddie and I preach, teach, lead worship or do whatever needs to be done—all under the Anointing of the Holy Spirit. Without Him, we are nothing!

The Wedding Day Prophecy

Benny Hinn's wife Suzanne's grandmother; Lil Skinn gave Eddie and me a prophecy via a note on our Wedding Day in 1977. My father-in-law said that Lil used to see the prophecies like a scroll unwinding. The card was addressed to Mr. & Mrs. E. Cain—To read on your "honeymoon". Inside it said:

November 5th 1977
A day to be remembered.
Your Wedding Day.

One seeks to find appropriate words
on this day of all days. And
Here is what the Lord says:-
"From this day— will I bless
you...and I will take thee My
servants—and will make you
as "signets"..(Those who leave
impressions of Christ) for
"I have chosen you"!

Lil Skinn

The beautiful paper Lil wrote the note on had a scripture on the bottom. 1 Kings 8:56 "There hath not failed one word of all His good promises." We later found out that Lil used to preach on the street corners with Smith Wigglesworth. She was truly an anointed and appointed woman of God!

To me the most interesting part of this Wedding Day note is that we did not even remember reading the note the day we opened all of our gifts. Six hundred people attended our wedding and many of the gifts were separated from their cards. God had instructed Eddie and me to pioneer our first church in 1988. We had only received our first stage of the ministerial licensing process. We would not have qualified to pioneer a church with The Assemblies of God without a special exception. We thought that we had "an out" and would not have to obey God's direction. God had the last laugh. It only took one phone call and a meeting with the sectional committee and we had their one hundred percent approval! The weekend of our "Grand Opening" I was looking in my closet for something and a Bible with my maiden name on it fell off the shelf—almost hitting me in the head—and Lil's note fell out of the Bible. It was just one more in a series of confirmations that we were in the center of God's will by pioneering the church.

How Hungry Are You?

Are you hungry for the things of God? If so, how hungry are you? Are you willing to allow the Holy Spirit to not only touch you, but to use you to ignite other's lives? Many of these "manifestations" of the Anointing are a sign and wonder to the unbeliever and believer alike [1 Corinthians 14:22 AMP]! I have been in a church meeting where someone else yielded to the Holy Spirit and had an unusual manifestation. It was as if someone had lit a piece of dynamite in the room. Bondages seemed to be broken off others as one person yielded to the Holy Spirit. The complete atmosphere of the place shifted into a higher gear, so to speak. Therefore, our obedience to yield to the Holy Spirit most likely will not effect only our lives, but others lives as well.

The first time I met Bill Caughell, he was directing the choir at Calvary Assembly. He has held many ministerial positions over the years and he recently shared this wonderful testimony with me [Kathryn Kuhlman was a Healing Evangelist]:

"When I was in High School and I am 75 years old today, Kathryn Kuhlman came to our church to minister. My friend from high school, Stanley Nelson's grandmother was in the hospital. She had been ill for twelve years, but had great faith! Stanley's grandmother called an ambulance to take her to the meeting. She told the ambulance driver, "You don't need to wait for me because I'll be able to take care of myself." The ambulance driver refused to listen to her and waited anyway. They rolled Stanley's grandmother's bed to the front left side of the church. After Kathryn was done preaching she called for a healing line. People lined up all across the front of the church. Kathryn Kuhlman started praying on the opposite side of the building from Stanley's grandmother. When Kathryn prayed for Stanley's grandmother, she was totally healed and got up from the ambulance bed floating at least one inch above the floor as she went up and down the aisles! Her feet never touched the ground. She lived for twelve more years. Once you see that you never doubt the power of God!"

My husband has had several of these types of manifestations. Eddie said that I would never see him dance or run in church. Never say never! Eddie has done both and then some! Before God touched us in a Rodney Howard-Browne meeting in 1993 at Carpenters Home Church, in Lakeland, Florida, Eddie was extremely shy and had to have every hair in place and his tie just right. In fact, Eddie was so shy that during the first year and a half of our first Pastorate, he would have diarrhea at the very thought of getting up in front of people and speaking. When God got His grip on us, we've truly never been the same again! It would take much too long to document the journey God has taken us on, so I am going to share a few highlights.

We were doing a Sunday through Friday, 10 AM and 7 PM Revival at Pastors Chuck and Barbara Farina, Sr.'s church, Abundant Life Fellowship, in Bozeman, Montana. Abundant Life Fellowship was the TBN affiliate for the area. It was the Monday morning service so the Television cameras were not on. How I wish they had been, because a picture is worth a thousand words! It was during the prayer time that I started on one side of the church praying for people and Eddie started on the other side of the church to pray for the people. Eddie said, "I knew something was going to happen, but I thought I was just going to spin because that had happed before. I felt a strange sensation, then landed on my feet and then fell out under the power of the Holy Spirit. I did not know what happened until someone told me that I had done a complete 360-degree backwards flip." At the time Eddie's weight was way up there and he was not in shape at all. I call it a sign and a wonder! By the time I saw Eddie, his glasses, wallet and change were spread out all over the place. Just a side note, Eddie did not get hurt. That is another sign and wonder!

If you were to interview some of the people who seemingly had a "strange" manifestation such as running around the entire building while sounding like a fire alarm, they would tell you that chains broke off of them as they yielded to the Holy Spirit! I've seen shy introverted people suddenly jump out of their chair, do a Holy Ghost jig and then collapse on the floor. The entire meeting went up to a higher level through their YIELDING to the Holy Spirit! I, on the other hand am basically an extrovert. While leading praise and worship with my husband, I began to prophesy and at the end of the prophecy stood there frozen with the microphone in my hand for the rest of the service. Just the fact that I did not speak was a sign and wonder to my husband and anyone else who knows me!

I have also been in some meetings where the manifestations of the Holy Spirit were so wild that I thought, "There is no way an unbeliever will get saved tonight." Then watch 300 people give their lives to Jesus Christ in that very same service! The Bible does say that signs and wonders are for the unbeliever and I am a witness to this truth! Think about it. How crazy was it in Acts 2 on the Day of Pentecost? Obviously, the people thought the 120 who came out of the Upper Room into the streets were drunk or Peter would not have had to stand up and say, *"These men are not drunk, as you suppose. It's only nine in the morning* [Acts 2:15]*!"* Do drunken people "speak in tongues"? No, they reel about, cannot walk a straight line, they laugh, they cry, and they may slobber all over you! The people would not have said these people are drunk if the 120 who came out of the Upper Room were only speaking in other tongues! The 120 obviously had other manifestations of the Anointing!

We Leak!

John 15:4-5 AMP
4 Dwell in Me, and I will dwell in you. [Live in Me,
and I will live in you.] Just as no branch can bear
fruit of itself without abiding in (being vitally united
to) the vine, neither can you

bear fruit unless you abide in Me.
5 I am the Vine; you are the branches. Whoever
lives in Me and I in him bears much (abundant)
fruit. However, apart from Me [cut off from vital
union with Me] you can do nothing.

WE LEAK. What do I mean by "we leak"? Well one touch of the Anointing will not be enough to last you a lifetime if you do not continue to "dwell" in the Anointing. The "Anointing" must become our dwelling place. You can lose the sense of "the experience" of the Anointing before you get into the parking lot! Our cars need oil [Anointing] added periodically and at other times our cars need a complete oil change because the oil has gotten old and nasty. The same is true of our being anointed and flowing in the Anointing! I have found that when I am abiding in the Anointing it does not matter how many aggravating and troublesome things are surrounding me, I can just laugh them off. I am not even affected by them. But as the Anointing begins to wane, I begin to get troubled by the troubles. Then if I go too long without living or dwelling in the Anointing, I can get downright nasty! We all need a complete oil change periodically! Stop right now and ask God for an oil change. Ask Him for "Fresh Oil"! Now receive it and thank Him for it!

Ephesians 5:18 AMP
18 And do not get drunk with wine, for that is
debauchery; but ever be filled and stimulated with
the [Holy] Spirit.

When Ephesians 5:18 says, "but ever be filled", it means "be being filled". The concept is of a continuous filling. We must be continually be, being filled with and controlled by the Holy Spirit. The saying, "A little dab will do you." does not work when you are going after The Anointing! The

Anointing is not a one-time experience. Living daily in His Presence is key to staying in The Anointing!

How can we "ever be filled and stimulated with the Holy Spirit"? The answer is by waiting on the Lord. By abiding in Him and continually staying in His Presence!

Isaiah 40:31 AMP
31 But those who wait for the Lord [who expect, look for, and hope in Him] shall change and renew their strength and power; they shall lift their wings and mount up [close to God] as eagles [mount up to the sun]; they shall run and not be weary, they shall walk and not faint or become tired.

What does it mean to "wait for the Lord"? According to the Greek "But those who wait for" means:

OT:6960 qavah (kaw-vaw'); a primitive root; to bind together (perhaps by twisting), i.e. collect; (figuratively) to expect:
KJV - gather (together), look, patiently, tarry, wait (for, on, upon). [1]

Notice in the Greek definition of "But those who wait for" it says, "to bind together, perhaps by twisting.[2] Similar to braided hair, it is woven together so that you cannot tell where one strand starts and the other strand lets off. That is what God wants for us. God wants your characteristics to be so much like His that you are a direct representative of Him! People will begin to see you and God as one unit.

The Greek definition of "But those who wait for" also says, "to wait on, to wait upon". [3] This depicts a servant, similar to a waiter or waitress in a restaurant. Therefore, waiting upon the Lord is serving the Lord or ministering to the Lord. The best way to minister to the Lord is to give Him praise and worship Him with all your heart, soul, mind and strength!

When you are feeling out of sorts, spend time with God. If I don't spend quality time with God everyday, I don't like myself and you would not like me either! At the first sign of feeling weary, spend some extra time with God. This is a sure cure to not end up having a melt down!

I can hear some of you saying right now, "I don't have time every day to spend time in prayer. It's easy for you to say, you don't know what my schedule looks like. I don't have any private place to go and pray. There is always someone around."

I remember hearing a story about Susanna Wesley, the mother of John and Charles Wesley. John Wesley was known for being the founder of the Methodist movement. Susanna Wesley was raising and home schooling nine children. With the task of running a household and home schooling nine children, I heard that Susanna would take her apron and pull it over her head to pray. The children knew when they saw their mother with her apron over her head that she was praying and they were not to disturb her. Her apron became her prayer closet. This particular story stuck with me as it made me aware that every one of us has enough time every day to spend some quality time with God! It is more about "want to" than the "ability" to do so. It's more about "knowing" the importance of spending time with God. I have come to realize that my prayer time is more for me than it is for God! I currently have an apron that a sweet woman of God, Helga Powell, gave me years ago after I shared this story during a sermon. Every time I look at the apron it reminds me of Susanna Wesley, Helga Powell, and the fact that we all have some time during each day to spend time with God!

1 Chronicles 16:11 AMP
Seek the Lord and His strength; yearn for and seek
His face and to be in His presence continually!

John 4:23-24 AMP
23 A time will come, however, indeed it is already
here, when the true (genuine) worshipers will
worship the Father in spirit and in truth (reality);
for the Father is seeking just such people
as these as His worshipers.
24 God is a Spirit (a spiritual Being) and those who
worship Him must worship Him in spirit and in
truth (reality).

To seek God's face and not His hand is extremely important when we spend time with God. How would you like it if every time your child, spouse, or friend came to spend time with you they only wanted to ask you for something? They did not truly come to spend time with you. They just wanted something from you. Although we serve a God that is loving and generous and wants to bless us more then we can imagine He desires our fellowship above all other things! He desires us to worship Him in spirit and in truth. He sees our heart and desires a sincere heart of worship! I love just spending time with God. I love being in His Presence! It is addicting! I just heard God say, that He loves spending time with me too! He would love to spend time with you as well!

Labels Can Cause A Leak

My husband and I along with our two children Jennifer and Eric traveled for three years [1995-1998] as Evangelists. Our ministry is a bit unusual in the fact that Eddie and I are both ordained, we alternate preaching and we do our own praise and worship. Many people told us that we could not do the music and the preaching, that is not the way it is done. They said that we would burn out. If God tells you to do the music as well as the preaching, not only can you do the music as well as the preaching, but it will be done with the Holy Spirit's Anointing all over it!

During our time as Evangelists, we were doing two services a day for six days a week. Not only did we do the music and the preaching [Eddie and I alternated preaching/ teaching], I was also home schooling our two children Jennifer and Eric. Admittedly, my daughter Jen was a big help with the home schooling. Both Jen and Eric received full academic college scholarships—one hundred percent tuition and money towards books to any Florida State College! Don't let people, whether well meaning or not, talk you out of what God has told you to do or how God tells you to do it! I firmly believe that we would not have been as effective or of no effect at all if we had listened to the naysayers instead of listening to God! To this day, we still have people who try to "label" us. Maybe you've had the same thing happen to you. "I see you more as an evangelist" or "I see you as a worship leader". The only thing we need to concern ourselves with is what God says we are. What ministry gift we operate in can change as the Spirit wills!

I can attest to the fact that each office has a different Anointing. When I stand in a pulpit as an Evangelist, I have a greater healing and salvation Anointing upon me. When I stand in the office of a Pastor, I have a greater desire and Anointing to see people grow and mature in the things of God. When I stand in the office of Worship Leader, I desire to see people come into a greater awareness of God's Presence. Walking in the wrong "office" or Anointing is no different than King Saul trying to get young David to wear his armor. King Saul's armor worked for King Saul. King Saul's armor did not fit David and it probably would have gotten David killed by Goliath [See 1 Samuel 17:38-39]! David was not just a shepherd. David was a worshiper, psalmist, warrior, shepherd and a King, to name a few titles. Don't let others put you in a box and then put a label on the box! No person can hear God for you better than you can hear God for yourself!

John 10:10 AMP
10 The thief comes only in order to steal and kill
and destroy. I came that they may have and enjoy
life, and have it in abundance
(to the full, till it overflows).

Matt 10:16 AMP
16 Behold, I am sending you out like sheep in the
midst of wolves; be wary and wise as serpents,
and be innocent (harmless, guileless, and without
falsity) as doves.

Matt 10:21-26 NIV
21 "Brother will betray brother to death, and a
father his child; children will rebel against their
parents and have them put to death. 22 All men will
hate you because of me, but he who stands firm to
the end will be saved. 23 When you are persecuted
in one place, flee to another. I tell you the truth,
you will not finish going through the cities of Israel
before the Son of Man comes.
24 "A student is not above his teacher, nor a servant
above his master. 25 It is enough for the student to
be like his teacher, and the servant like his master.
If the head of the house has been called Beelzebub,
how much more the members of his household!
26 "So do not be afraid of them. There is nothing
concealed that will not be disclosed, or hidden that
will not be made known.

Satan's entire task is to steal from you, kill you and destroy you. If he can't stop you from being a Christian, he will try and stop your effectiveness. He will try to put a wrong label on you to slow you down or even kill you if he can. He has the art of nagging perfected. He is a liar and the father of lies [John 8:44]! The devil does not play fair. He often times uses those closest to you to steal, kill and destroy you. He will often use your "brethren" to try and stop you. The best way to keep things in perspective is that when people reject you, remember that they are not rejecting you, but they are rejecting God.

Operating in the Anointing of the Holy Spirit stirs things up! If you were looking into a large barrel of water it could look pure and clean. If you then took a stick and stirred the water in the barrel up, all of the debris that had settled on the bottom would begin to surface and you would then see the true state of the water. That is exactly what happens when revival or the Anointing comes into a place. What once looked just fine now begins to show its imperfections. I personally had this experience when God touched me so mightily in Rodney Howard-Browne's Carpenter's Home Lakeland, Florida Revival in 1993. The closer I moved toward God's Presence, the more I realized the dirt that had settled down on the bottom of my life. You cannot face a holy God, draw closer and closer into His Presence and not begin to see the true you! The great news is that when God brings these imperfections to our attention, He then will take them away as we yield ourselves completely to Him. I personally believe that is why God uses the Holy laughter. It is like a sedative while He is doing surgery.

It is the people who will not admit they are in need and who will not yield to God, who many times become the greatest opponents to God and His Presence. They, like Saul before he became Paul will persecute the move of God and think they are doing the work of God [See Acts 7:58—9:22].

Eph 3:19 AMP
19[That you may really come] to know [practi-
cally, through experience for yourselves] the
love of Christ, which far surpasses mere knowl-
edge [without experience]; that you may be filled
[through all your being] unto all the fullness of
God [may have the richest measure of the divine
Presence, and become a body wholly filled and
flooded with God Himself]

It was always a joy to be in a church where the people and the pastor truly wanted as much of God's Presence as they could possibly have! Unfortunately, we would find a group of very hungry for God people and a not so hungry pastor or a very hungry pastor and a not so hungry congregation. We've often wondered if there was a way to unite the hungry congregations with the hungry pastors. We are not waiting on God. He is waiting on us. God wants every one, everywhere to walk in His fullness!

If God asks you to do something, the minute you obey He equips you for the task. Do not say, "I am too young. I am too old. I am too fat. I am too skinny. I stutter when I speak. I do not have the adequate finances. I am too educated. I am not educated enough. I am too shy. I am not talented. I can't sing. I can't preach. I can't teach. I'm pregnant. What about my children? I cannot play an instrument. The list could go on and on. If God says you can, you can! Take a look at Gideon.

Judges 6:11-12; 14-16 AMP
11 Now the Angel of the Lord came and sat under
the oak (terebinth) at Ophrah, which belonged to
Joash the Abiezrite, and his son Gideon was beating
wheat in the winepress to hide it
from the Midianites.

*12 And the Angel of the Lord appeared to him and said to him, **The Lord is with you, you mighty man of [fearless] courage.***
14 The Lord turned to him and said, Go in this your might, and you shall save Israel from the hand of Midian. Have I not sent you?
*15 Gideon said to Him, Oh Lord, how can I deliver Israel? Behold, **my clan is the poorest in Manasseh, and I am the least in my father's house.***
16 The Lord said to him, Surely I will be with you, and you shall smite the Midianites as one man.
[Bolded emphasis mine]

Gideon was hiding in the winepress to beat his wheat because he was afraid of the Midianites. Gideon was convinced that his family clan was the poorest and he was the least in his father's house. Self-esteem does not get much lower than that! God, however, saw Gideon much differently. God called Gideon, "You mighty man of fearless courage". God saw Gideon as Israel's deliverer.

What is God saying about you? The devil does not want you to know what God is saying about you. The devil does not want you to see how God sees you. I received an email that had a list of things for people to begin praying over themselves (and their ministries if applicable). One of the prayers I began to pray is:

"God, I ask You to show me what the enemy does not want me to see. Give me discernment. I ask You to allow me to be seen as You see me, not as the enemy wants me to be seen."

As a result of praying this prayer, God recently allowed a "Divine Connection" through a former church member, Lora

Votaw. Lora found out that her current Pastor, Pastor Russ Benson, who pastors Covenant Community Fellowship in Indiana, met my husband and me when he was a teenager during a revival in 1998. Lora wrote and said that Pastor Russ told her that to this day they still refer to the 1998 Calvary Assembly of God, Port Charlotte, Florida revival as "The Cain Revival". Pastor Russ went on to the Brownsville School of Ministry. We could have gone our entire lifetime without ever meeting Pastor Russ and hearing his story. Pastor Russ was a best friend with Calvary Assembly's Pastor Kolenda's son and shares this story.

God moved in a mighty way at Calvary A/G in 1998. I just returned back from the Brownsville Revival with some of the youth and I was so hungry for a move of the Holy Spirit at our church. When we heard that there was going to be an evangelist at the church we were full of expectation. Honestly, when we first saw the Cain's our expectations were lowered a bit. They were not flashy preachers, they did not yell or even try to stir up the crowd. They were very simple. Yet, as they began to worship you could sense the atmosphere change. What a powerful Anointing ushered into the church. The services were all marked with a rich and deep sense of God's glory! My life was touched in a powerful way, as were many people in attendance. I can remember being so drunk in the Holy Spirit that I had to be carried out at the end of the evening. They also did services at the school of the church. I never saw so many youth so dramatically touched by God's Presence. School had to be cancelled the rest of the day because the children were under the power of God. So many kids were touched; they were nearly piled on top of one another. They were laughing, crying, and soaking in God's glory. We had to explain to several parents what was happening to their children because they were not used to seeing the manifestation of the Presence of God. It was a glorious season of God's Presence. We still talk about it to this day. God used the Cain's in a powerful way in my life and many who were in attendance. I have been ruined by the Presence of God. More Lord!

If we had listened to the devil, we would have never stepped out in obedience to God to evangelize. We would have never operated in the Anointing to be an "evangelist", as well as "evangelistic worship leaders". How many lives would not have been reached if we had decided to stay put as pastors who also lead worship? What if we would have succumbed to only being "pastors" and turned the worship over to others? In our case many of the miracles that take place, take place during the worship portion of the service.

I can remember preaching in Yulee, Florida at an Assemblies of God Church. We were having tremendous Holy Ghost and Fire services that week! As I was preaching, a man raised his hand like he wanted to ask a question. I had learned by experience it is usually never a good idea to acknowledge a person who wanted to ask a question at the preaching portion of the service. I just continued preaching as if I had not seen his hand raised. Many times the devil will use a sincere person with a genuine question to disrupt the flow of the service. There is a time for everything. The man then stood up and walked out of the building. I thought, "I guess he is upset that I did not acknowledge him." I continued to preach the message the Holy Spirit had given me for the evening. The man came back into the building and went up to where the pastor was sitting and said something to the pastor. Finally, the pastor asks if he could interrupt to share something. I gave the microphone to the pastor and he shared the man's testimony. I cannot remember the man's name, so we will refer to him as Joe. Pastor said Joe had been injured at the nearby missile making facility where he had worked. His shoulder had been crushed and was frozen. He could not raise his arm up due to the injury. While I was preaching, the healing Anointing fell upon him and he realized that he could raise his hand. I now realized that he was not trying to ask a question, but was realizing that he was healed. He was so excited about being healed that he went out of the building to the children's church building where his daughter was teaching the children and showed her how he could not only raise his arm, but make a complete circle with his arm. His daughter filled with joy said, "You need to go and tell the pastor."

As Paul Harvey says, "And now for the rest of the story." The next day Joe went to the doctor to show the doctor that he was healed. The doctor took x-rays and said you still have the same problem in your shoulder that you previously had. You are not healed. Joe said to the doctor, "You mean I cannot do this [as he raised his hand above his head] or that [as he made a circular motion with his arm]?" The doctor told Joe that he did not know how Joe was doing what was medically impossible. I add, "Miracles still happen today!" Joe was a walking sign and wonder!

Understand that if God's label for us for the season was "pastors", then we would have been more effective as "pastors"! If God has a special Anointing upon Eddie and me to do both the praise and worship and the preaching portion of the service, then no one else could do a better job in that particular service. The same thing holds true for you! If God's label for you for this season is "a stay at home mom", then no one can do a better job than you! If God's label for you is "lawyer" for this season, then no one can do a better job than you! Remember, one label is not "better" or "greater" than another as far as God is concerned. God just requires obedience to His will!

What is God saying to you? How does God see you? Begin to ask God to show you what the enemy does not want you to see. Ask God to give you discernment. Ask God to allow you to be seen as He sees you, not as the enemy wants you to be seen." Believe what God tells you and shows you! Act upon what God tells you and shows you. I believe we are all miracles of God waiting to happen!

One Touch Is Not Enough For A Lifetime

We were ministering in a church in Hollywood, Florida. During the first service, which happened to be a Sunday morning, as Eddie and I were doing Praise and Worship, the Lord, gave me a word of knowledge that someone's left ear was being healed. To my surprise [she had not mentioned the problem to me] it turned out to be Pastor Linda's left ear and since we were staying in Pastor Linda's home, one lady [the Women's Ministries Leader and 3rd Generation Pentecostal] began to tell people that it was a set up. My first thought was, if I were going to plan a "set up" for a healing, it would be much more spectacular than a left ear! Well as the service continued, this Women's Ministry Leader began to have demonic manifestations. After everyone else had left, we prayed for her. She began to manifest in an even greater manner. In fact, she dug her fingernails into my arms so deeply that I should have been bleeding, but I did not receive the tiniest mark on my arms! Then the demon began speaking through her, "We won't let her go". At that time my husband and I had been holding revival services around America with a service schedule of Sunday through Friday, 10 A.M. and 7 PM and needless to say we were living in the Anointing and loving it. As the demons continued saying, "We won't let her go", I instantly began laughing because

I knew they had to go and what a joke to try and tell us otherwise! Just a side note, if you really want to make satan angry, just laugh at him. It drives him crazy! I'm telling you nothing can truly disturb you for long if you will stay in the Anointing!

Bottom line, the woman was set free. She did not even look like the same lady when we saw her the very next service! She had the glow of the Lord upon her and was totally free! Pastor Linda's ear had oil pouring out of it for the rest of the day and was totally and completely healed! My husband and I would not have been able to be the vessels the Holy Spirit used to minister to either of them, had we not continually been being filled with the Holy Spirit and His Anointing!

I believe one of the main reasons we see people in church circles who are supposedly born again and Spirit-filled yet they are the meanest, most ornery people—certainly not Christ like—is due to the fact that these people had a one time experience and never "walked in the Spirit". Or they leaked from the last infilling! We must continually be being filled with and controlled by the Holy Spirit! It's Christ in us the hope of glory.

Is It Time For A Holy Ghost Oil Change?

Sometimes we need a complete oil change in the Spirit! My mom's dad was a mechanic and he said the best way to maintain your car's engine was to change the oil every 3,000 miles. The oil gets debris in it and gets less efficient through use. Without proper oil changes, you can destroy the engine of a vehicle. The same is true of our being anointed by the Holy Spirit. We need to take ourselves off the road of life for a time of refreshing—an oil change. I suggest going to a weeklong or a long weekend Spirit-filled meeting some-where, where you can come away from everyday life and sit and soak up the Holy Spirit's Presence! My husband and I are ruined. Our idea of a vacation is to go and soak in The River of God at some Holy Spirit filled camp meeting for a week or so. We cannot think of anywhere else we want to be. Even though we have lived in the Orlando, Florida area that has been called "The Vacation Capital of the World!" for the greater part of our lives, we would rather be in a Holy Spirit meeting!

Now, I am not saying you shouldn't go and take a vacation at Disney World, the beach or whatever else interests you. Although, I bet a lot of you would concur with me that most of the time you need a vacation from your vacation. On the other hand, you can go and spend a week or weekend in a Holy Ghost anointed meeting and you will come away with a new and fresh zeal, vision, peace, joy and just plain feel great and refreshed!

You may be saying to yourself right now, "A vacation of any kind is not in my foreseeable future". Well, I have great news for you! Remember Jude verse 20? You can build yourself up by simply praying in the Holy Spirit wherever you are! I will give you a little hint: it is when you least "feel" like praying in the Spirit that you NEED to pray in the Holy Spirit! Try it. You'll like it! I would suggest putting some Holy Spirit anointed worship music on in the background. You can contact me for some truly anointed worship music at www.BeckyFarinaCain.com. Wait until everyone is in bed and lay in His Presence! The Holy Spirit will show you a creative way(s) to get alone with Him. How about sneaking out to your car to be alone? Remember Susannah Wesley put her apron over her head to be alone with God. If you take one step towards God, He will come running to you!

Jude 20 AMP
20 But you, beloved, build yourselves up
[founded] on your most holy faith

[make progress, rise like an edifice higher and higher], praying in the Holy Spirit;

Jude 20 says speaking in tongues builds us up and we make progress, raising like a structure higher and higher! It is not a one-time experience…it is a moment by moment infilling! How many of you eat a wonderful meal and try to go on the strength of that one meal for three months or more? You would be six feet under in a coffin somewhere if you tried to eat one meal to sustain you for three months! Just as our physical bodies need water and food, so do our spirits and souls need the spiritual nourishment and refreshment of being filled with the Holy Spirit!

As we stay continuously filled and immersed in the Holy Spirit, we become like a saturated sponge that will spread to anyone we touch around us. Let's face it; we are more than likely going to ooze something on people. It is much better for others and ourselves when we ooze the Holy Spirit wherever we go!

CHAPTER ELEVEN

KEY # 7—THE ANOINTING IS TRANSFERABLE

The Principle Thing

2 Corinthians 1:21 AMP
21 But it is God Who confirms and makes us
steadfast and establishes us [in joint fellowship]
with you in Christ, and has consecrated and
anointed us [enduing us with the gifts of
the Holy Spirit];

The principle thing about "The Transference of the Anointing" is **it is God Who anoints us**! He is the Anointer and we are the anointed! Without God, there is no Anointing! If we read 2 Corinthians 1:21 remembering that Christ means "The Anointed One and His Anointing", then the passage would read like this:

21 But it is God Who confirms and makes us
steadfast and establishes us [in joint fellowship]
with you in Christ—the Anointed One and His

Anointing, and has consecrated and anointed us
[enduing us with the gifts of the Holy Spirit];

It is of utmost importance that you remember that **God is the One Who anoints us,** while reading this chapter! It is God Who does the healing! After God anoints a person, then that person can transfer the Anointing to cloth, another person, or an object. We must follow the leading of the Holy Spirit when operating under His Anointing. It is "as the Spirit wills", not as we will [1 Corinthians 12:11]. What does that mean? It means that the Holy Spirit is the One who determines who, what, when and where. It means that just as Jesus only did what the Father did, we too should only do what the Father tells us to do [John 5:19].

Can The Anointing Be Transferred Via Electronics?

Have you ever seen an old 1940's tent revival clip of Oral Roberts and sensed the same healing Anointing in your living room as was taking place in the tent revival years ago? Have you ever watched an old video of a revival meeting and the same Anointing that was present at the meeting you attended, comes upon you every time you watch it? You have probably "transferred" it to a DVD by now. All puns intended. Transferring the information on a video to a DVD or transferring the information from a cassette tape to a CD are wonderful illustrations of what it means to "transfer" the Anointing. Does the original cassette tape lose the information when you transfer it to a CD? No. The information is now on both the cassette tape and CD. You could then decide to transfer the information from the CD to your iPod. Now you have the same information on the cassette tape, CD, and your iPod. The same Anointing that was in the revival meeting and on the video of the revival meeting is now on the DVD or any other media you transferred it to.

Have you ever watched a replay of a television program that was aired weeks earlier and yet the prophetic word coming forth was a now word for you and your current circumstances? What about a preaching cassette from years ago that ministered healing to you today? Have you ever listened to a CD, DVD or iPod of the song and musicians that ministered healing to you and were enraptured with the same Anointing that took place when God ministered healing to you? Why is that?

God is not confined to time and space as we understand time and space. Once the Anointing is upon a speaker, singer, or musician, the Anointing is transferred through whatever medium is being used to record the event. The same healing Anointing that is present in a meeting, if captured on tape, CD, iPod, Camcorder, cell phone, internet or DVD, will be present on the tape, CD, iPod, Camcorder, cell phone, internet or DVD. The Anointing is transferable! The more electronics that are created, the more avenues we have to spread the Anointing.

Old Testament Transference Through Cloth

1 Kings 19:15-21 AMP
15 And the Lord said to him, Go, return on your
way to the Wilderness of Damascus; and when you
arrive, anoint Hazael to be king over Syria.
16 And anoint Jehu son of Nimshi to be king over
Israel, and anoint Elisha son of Shaphat of
Abel-meholah to be prophet in your place.
17 And him who escapes from the sword of Hazael
Jehu shall slay, and him who escapes the
sword of Jehu Elisha shall slay.
18 Yet I will leave Myself 7,000 in Israel, all the
knees that have not bowed to Baal and every mouth
that has not kissed him.

139

*19 So Elijah left there and found Elisha son of
Shaphat, whose plowing was being done with
Twelve yoke of oxen, and he drove the twelfth.
Elijah crossed over to him and cast
his mantle upon him.
20 He left the oxen and ran after Elijah and said,
Let me kiss my father and mother, and then I will
follow you. And he [testing Elisha] said, Go on
back. What have I done to you?
[Settle it for yourself.]
21 So Elisha went back from him. Then he took a
yoke of oxen, slew them, boiled their flesh with the
oxen's yoke [as fuel], and gave to the people, and
they ate. Then he arose, followed Elijah, and served
him. [2 Kings 3:11.]*

What is a mantle? According to Nelson's Illustrated Bible Dictionary, a mantle was the distinctive Hebrew outer garment made of two pieces of thick woolen material sewn together, with slits rather than sleeves for the arms. The typical Hebrew slept on the floor with his mantle used as a covering to keep him warm. A handy one-piece garment, the mantle protected a person from the weather. Because it fitted loosely, it could also be used to conceal or carry items.[1] Therefore, a mantle is basically a piece of cloth.

Elijah's mantle was the "anointed cloth object" used for the transference of the Anointing from Elijah to Elisha. Once Elijah cast his mantle on Elisha, Elisha had a choice at that very moment to either receive the Anointing or to reject the Anointing. He had the choice to either answer God's call into ministry or to refuse God's calling him into ministry.

Elisha not only answered God's call into ministry, but he burned his plowing equipment. Elisha's plowing equipment was his means of making money. We can learn a lot from Elisha. He used the equipment he needed for his livelihood to burn a "sacrifice to God" as a means of consecrating and setting himself apart for service to the Lord. Elisha gave one hundred percent!

Elisha found out that you must be tenacious to receive what God has for you. Even though the Children of Israel were promised "The Promise Land", they still had to "Go and Possess the Land" [See Joshua 1]! They were guaranteed victory, but only if they fought for what was theirs. Too many times we think, "Well, God said this is mine, so I'll just sit here and wait for it to jump on me!" No! We need to fight with everything that is within us knowing that we win!

2 Kings 2:9-14 AMP
9 And when they had gone over, Elijah said to
Elisha, Ask what I shall do for you before I am
taken from you. And Elisha said, I pray you, let a
double portion of your spirit be upon me.
10 He said, You have asked a hard thing. However,
if you see me when I am taken from you, it shall be
so for you—but if not, it shall not be so.
11 As they still went on and talked, behold, a chariot
of fire and horses of fire parted the two of them, and
Elijah went up by a whirlwind into heaven.
12 And Elisha saw it and he cried, My father, my
father! The chariot of Israel and its horsemen! And
he saw him no more. And he took hold of his own
clothes and tore them in two pieces.
13 He took up also the mantle of Elijah that fell
from him and went back and stood by
the bank of the Jordan.
14 And he took the mantle that fell from Elijah and
struck the waters and said, Where is the Lord, the
God of Elijah? And when he had struck the waters,
they parted this way and that, and Elisha went over.

Even though Elijah had already transferred the Anointing of ministry to Elisha, Elisha knew that there was more. When the Lord was about to take Elijah up to heaven by a whirlwind, Elijah told Elisha three times during that day to stay put [2 Kings 2]. Elisha refused to leave Elijah! The other prophets kept discouraging Elisha. We need the same kind of persistence Elisha had when we are dealing with the Anointing of God. There is always more! Elisha's tenacity paid off. Second Kings 2:9 says that Elisha would receive a "double portion" of Elijah's spirit when and if Elisha saw Elijah go up in a whirlwind. Elisha stayed with Elijah until he watched Elijah go up in a whirlwind. Elijah's mantle fell upon Elisha and Elisha received the double portion Anointing!

Elisha found out that there is a double blessing in store when you tie into and serve someone who is anointed by God. Elisha not only "received" the double portion of Elijah's Anointing, but Elisha immediately put the Anointing to work by striking the waters with Elijah's mantle and parting the water to walk on dry ground. This one act showed the others that Elijah's anointed mantle and ministry had indeed transferred to Elisha. The fact that Elisha performed twice as many miracles as Elijah did is another evidence that Elisha had received a double portion of Elijah's Anointing.

The Anointing Can Transfer Into Our Physical Bones

2 Kings 13:20-21 AMP
20 Elisha died, and they buried him. Bands of the
Moabites invaded the land in the spring
of the next year.
21 As a man was being buried [on an open bier],
such a band was seen coming; and the man was
cast into Elisha's grave. And when the man being let
down touched the bones of Elisha,
he revived and stood on his feet.

Even after death, Elisha's dead bones still carried the Anointing. A dead man was thrown into Elisha's tomb. When the body touched Elisha's bones, the man came to life and stood up on his feet. That proves that The Anointing can permeate our physical body whether dead or alive.

New Testament Transference Through Cloth

Acts 19:11-12 AMP
11 And God did unusual and extraordinary miracles
by the hands of Paul,
12 So that handkerchiefs or towels or aprons which
had touched his skin were carried away and put
upon the sick, and their diseases left them and the
evil spirits came out of them.

Once again, we must remember that it is God Who anoints. Notice that Acts 19:11 says, "And GOD DID" unusual and extraordinary miracles by the hands of Paul. It was not Paul, but God working through Paul! God anointed Paul's hands, and God's Anointing through Paul transferred God's Anointing into cloth. The cloth then transferred the Anointing of healing to the people the cloth touched.

Hebrews 13:8 AMP
8 Jesus Christ (the Messiah) is [always] the same,
yesterday, today, [yes] and forever (to the ages).

Since God is still the same yesterday, today and forever, you and I under The Anointing and direction of the Holy Spirit can release God's Anointing into cloth, people and objects. We have seen two examples, one example of Elijah and Elisha in the Old Testament and the other example of Paul and the cloth in the New Testament. Now let's look at some modern day examples.

During one of our regular Sunday morning services, God instructed us to have any person in the congregation who had unsaved spouses or loved ones to bring in something that the person who was unsaved had regular contact with—like a pillowcase. Sunday night when they brought the objects, we would pray, lay hands upon and release the Anointing into the objects and watch God work in their lives. We just assumed that people were going to bring in cloth items.

To our great surprise one of the ladies who's husband was unsaved brought a twelve-pack of beer. Not a six-pack, but a twelve-pack of beer. We did not even know that they made a twelve-pack of beer. Boy, that will challenge how religious you are! The wife explained that the beer was the one thing her husband had the greatest regular contact with, since he was an alcoholic. As shocked as we were, we decided that if God could anoint a pillowcase, He could anoint beer. We proceeded to pray for the beer to make her husband ill and that he would stop drinking –and ultimately get saved. The wife came back the next week with an unusual report. Her husband went to the refrigerator as his custom was and got one of the "anointed beers". She said that he was yelling at her as usual and opened the "anointed beer" and all of the sudden, he told her, "Honey, I love you." The next thing that happened was he spit out the beer and said there must be something wrong with this beer. The same scenario was repeated until he finally decided that the beer must have been tainted and threw the rest of it out. The Anointing is absolutely transferable!

A different lady, whose spouse was not saved, brought in a pillowcase and we laid hands on the pillowcase and prayed that her husband would get saved. She put the pillowcase on her husband's pillow and the very first night he could not sleep. This went on for several nights. One evening as he found that he could not sleep again, he got up and turned on the television where he heard the gospel and prayed the sinner's prayer. The Anointing is transferable!

We've had many testimonies where prayer cloths that we've prayed over and laid hands upon releasing God's healing Anointing were sent out of state and abroad and as the person received the prayer cloth they were miraculously healed. The Anointing is transferable!

We have experienced sensing the Anointing as we were driving to an anointed meeting. The closer we got to the meeting, the stronger the Anointing we sensed. After being so radically touched and changed by the Holy Spirit in 1993 at Rodney-Howard-Browne's meetings at Carpenters Home Church, Lakeland, Florida, we experienced tremendous anointed services breaking out at the church we were pastoring. During this time we were running many extra services at the church. Countless people would tell us that as they were driving to our church, the closer they got to the church, the stronger they could feel the Anointing. I believe God's Anointing was permeating the parking lot, the chairs, the carpet and the building!

Eddie and I recently were asked to do a meeting at Pastors Ken and Dean Redman's church, Abundant Life Assembly of God, in Midland, Texas. Before church, we were brought into a special "prayer room" to pray before the service began. The moment I stepped foot into the room, a heavenly peace overtook me. I did not want to leave the room! You could definitely sense the Holy Spirit's Presence big time in that prayer room! Praise God that we did leave the room. If we hadn't, we wouldn't have gotten to be a part of touching the lives of the people God had for us to touch for Him that evening! The Anointing in the service was powerful!

Over the years, many people have come into our home (wherever that was at the time). I cannot count the times people would comment, "There is such a peace in your home". The "peace" they were sensing was the Presence of the Holy Spirit Anointing. Do not underestimate how God's Presence can fill your home or your workplace. Invite His Presence in. Decree that your home is filled with the Righteousness, Peace and Joy of the Holy Ghost. Watch as the atmosphere changes in your home.

I can hear some of you "saved" spouses who live with "unsaved" spouses complaining that this would work if you had a believing spouse. You do not need to have a believing spouse to bring the anointed Presence of God into your home. 1 John 4:4 tells us that, "He Who lives in you is greater [mightier] than he who is in the world." 1 Corinthians 7:14 informs us, the believing spouse sanctifies the unbelieving spouse and that results in your children being pure and clean. Unfortunately, too much credit and power has been given to the devil! You are on the winning side! Jesus living big on the inside of you is far greater than any devil!

1 Corinthians 7:14 AMP
14 For the unbelieving husband is set apart (separated, withdrawn from heathen contamination, and affiliated with the Christian people) by union with his consecrated (set-apart) wife, and the unbelieving wife is set apart and separated through union with her consecrated husband. Otherwise your children would be unclean (unblessed heathen, outside the Christian covenant), but as it is they are prepared for God [pure and clean].

The Doctrine of the Laying on of Hands

Hebrews 6:1-3 AMP
1 THEREFORE LET us go on and get past the elementary stage in the teachings and doctrine of Christ (the Messiah), advancing steadily toward the completeness and perfection that belong to spiritual

maturity. Let us not again be laying the foundation
of repentance and abandonment of dead works
(dead formalism) and of the faith
[by which you turned] to God,
2 With teachings about purifying, the laying on of
hands, the resurrection from the dead, and eternal
judgment and punishment. [These are all matters of
which you should have been fully
aware long, long ago.]
3 If indeed God permits, we will [now] proceed [to
advanced teaching]

Hebrews chapter six teaches us that "the doctrine of laying on of hands" is an elementary stage in the teachings and doctrine of Christ, The Messiah. Laying on of hands is one of the basic teachings we should have received after becoming a follower of Jesus.

One of the elementary teachings of "the doctrine of laying on of hands" is it is unwise to let just any person lay hands on you. You may not want what the other person is transferring. The upside is that you can plead the blood of Jesus over yourself and ask God to protect you in the event that someone tried to transfer something to you that is not of God! You do not need to be in fear. You just need to use wisdom.

Most large gatherings have an assigned and approved prayer team. The prayer team members usually wear a badge of some sort showing people that they have been given the authority to lay hands on people in prayer. Should you find yourself in a situation where someone you do not know and who does not have any badge indicating he/she is authorized to pray over you, starts to lay hands on you to pray, just stop them and say, "no thank you". It is not rude to decline prayer.

Mark 16:17-18 AMP
17 And these attesting signs will accompany
those who believe: in My name they will drive out
demons; they will speak in new languages;
18 They will pick up serpents; and [even] if they
drink anything deadly, it will not hurt them; they
will lay their hands on the sick,
and they will get well.

Are you a believer in Jesus Christ? Mark 16:17-18 lists the attesting signs that are to accompany a believer. One of those signs is that believers will lay hands on the sick and they will get well. Notice the Bible did not say in Mark chapter sixteen, "these attesting signs will only accompany a person in the fivefold ministry—apostles, prophets, evangelists, pastors and teachers [See Ephesians 4:11 regarding the fivefold ministry]. No, Ephesians 4:12 actually teaches us that the people in the fivefold ministry are God's gifts to the believers, to equip the believers to do the work of the ministry. This includes "the laying on of hands".

I can hear some people saying, "What if I lay hands on them and they don't get well or worse than that they get sicker or die?" The answer is, "What if they do get healed?" They were going to stay sick, get worse, or die anyway. You are not "the healer". God is! It is God's Healing Anointing flowing through you! Start asking yourself, "What if they do get healed?" I truthfully have never had any one turn me down when I asked if I could pray for them with one exception. One exception in thirty plus years is a pretty great track record! Most people are thrilled that anyone cares enough to pray for them. Try it. You'll like it!

Laying on of hands etiquette would be a profitable lesson for believers to learn! For instance, it is a good idea to ask the person who is in the need of prayer if they mind if you lay your hand on them to pray. I would also advise as much as it is possible that women pray with women and men pray with men. In my case, most of the time my husband and I try to pray together for people. Etiquette also includes using breath mints when you are praying for people. Bad breath can be a great distraction.

Many times in an anointed service, we will ask for people who would like prayer to come up to the front of the auditorium. Usually, the people are told what to expect after coming up to the front for prayer. An example of this is we might say, "Everyone who wants prayer, please come forward and line up in a single line, shoulder to shoulder facing the front of the auditorium. The ushers will assist you. I/we will be coming down the line to pray for each and everyone of you. Please remain in prayer as you wait for hands to be laid on you. Close your eyes and lift your hands to heaven. Be ready to receive from God the minute hands are laid on you. Please repeat this prayer. "Heavenly Father, the minute hands are laid on me, I will receive what you have for me. In the Name of Jesus, Amen." These instructions eliminate some of the fear of the unknown.

Healing is Transferred Through
The Laying on of Hands

Luke 4:40 AMP
40 Now at the setting of the sun [indicating the end
of the Sabbath], all those who had any [who were]
sick with various diseases brought them to Him, and
He laid His hands upon every one
of them and cured them.

Mark 8:23-25 AMP
23 And He caught the blind man by the hand and
led him out of the village; and when He had spit on

his eyes and put His hands upon him, He asked him,
Do you [possibly] see anything?
24 And he looked up and said, I see people, but
[they look] like trees, walking.
25 Then He put His hands on his eyes again; and
the man looked intently [that is, fixed his eyes on
definite objects], and he was restored and saw
everything distinctly [even what was at a distance].

Healing is transferred through the laying on of hands. In contrast to Luke 4:40 where every person Jesus laid hands on was healed, I find it interesting that Mark 8: 23-25 reveals that even Jesus had to administer the laying on of hands two times before the blind man received his complete eyesight. In this particular passage, Jesus even puts His spit on the blind mans eyes as a means of transferring healing. I don't think people would take too kindly to our spitting on them these days. Although, I guess if a person were sick enough or wanted to receive a healing badly enough they would let you spit on them. I certainly hope God does not ask me to spit on anyone. I can see it now. The First Church of the Spitting Anointing [Just kidding]. The bottom line is do not be afraid to lay hands on a person a second or even third time when praying for them.

Empty Hands On Empty Heads?

In order for the "laying on of hands" to be the most effective, the person who is laying hands upon [the giver] and the person having hands laid upon them [the receiver], both have to be in faith. It doesn't do any good to have "anointed" hands laid upon you if you are not willing to receive what God has for you! I have felt more power go out of me praying for a piece of equipment than I have praying for some people! It literally feels like the Anointing is coming back to you and it is. It is almost as if some people come for prayer with the attitude, "give it your best shot". With that attitude you might as well go back to your seat and sit down! We've had some of our catchers say, "If they don't take the Anointing, I will!" and down under the power of the Holy Spirit they go.

The opposite is true as well. I have been in a prayer line as the receiver of prayer and when the giver of prayer came and laid hands upon me, there was nothing transferred because the person did not walk in God's Anointing! You cannot give away what you do not have. Thank God that has been the exception and not the rule!

An Extraordinary Receiver

There was a woman in the Bible who had been subject to bleeding for twelve years and had spent all her money on doctors to only get worse. When she heard about Jesus, she came up from behind him in the crowd and touched his cloak because she thought, "If I just touch his clothes, I will be healed." Immediately her bleeding stopped and she felt in her body that she was freed from her suffering. The Bible says that at once Jesus realized that power had gone out from him. He turned around in the crowd and asked, "Who touched my clothes?" His disciples answered, "You see the people crowding against you, and yet you can ask, 'Who touched me?'" But Jesus kept looking around to see who had done it. Then the woman, knowing what had happened to her, came and fell at his feet and, trembling with fear, told him the whole truth. He said to her, "Daughter, your faith has healed you. Go in peace and be freed from your suffering [Mark 5:27-34 NIV]."

Mark 5:34 AMP
34 And He said to her, Daughter, your faith (your trust and confidence in Me, springing from faith in

*God) has restored you to health. Go in (into) peace
and be continually healed and freed from your
[distressing bodily] disease.*

Here is a woman who was a receiver! She believed in
the transference of the healing Anointing. Jesus told her,
"Daughter, your faith has restored you to health." Her faith!
This proves we must come for prayer in faith, trust and
confidence in God in order to receive all He has for us! This
woman was not only immediately healed; Jesus said she was
continually healed!

Falling Under The Power Of The Holy Spirit!

This is a funny and true story. We knew this young man
who had a real fear issue with falling down to the floor under
the power of the Holy Spirit. Although he had a tremendous
fear of falling, he also had a great hunger to experience what
he saw others experiencing. He confided in us that he had
gone home and practiced falling onto his bed over and over
again until he got enough nerve to trust God that he would
not get hurt. I give him credit for being tenacious! I have
heard someone say about fear, "Just do it afraid". I think that
is great advice!

Does falling under the power of the Holy Spirit make
one person more spiritual than another? Not as far as I know.
I have also had people tell me that some people who prayed
for them were so insistent that they fall under the power of
the Holy Spirit that they gave the person what they called a
"courtesy drop". I laughed. No one needs to give anyone a
"courtesy drop" either! Just relax, yield yourself to God and
if you go down under the power of the Holy Spirit enjoy it!
It is important to stay down on the floor until God is done
working on you.

Laying on of hands is not the only way Jesus healed people, but it is definitely one of the ways to transfer healing.

Invoking a Blessing Through Laying On Of Hands

Mark 10:16 AMP
16 And He took them [the children up one by one]
in His arms and [fervently invoked a] blessing,
placing His hands upon them.

We can invoke a blessing on people through the laying on of hands. In Mark 10:13, the disciples were scolding the parents for bringing their children to have Jesus lay hands on the children and invoke a blessing on them. Jesus let His disciples know to stop scolding the parents and to bring the little children to Him to be blessed. Jesus told the disciples that everyone must become like a little child in order to receive the Kingdom of God.

Ordination

2 Timothy 1:6 AMP
6 That is why I would remind you to stir up
(rekindle the embers of, fan the flame of, and keep
burning) the [gracious] gift of God, [the inner fire]
that is in you by means of the laying on of my hands
[with those of the elders at your ordination].

Laying on of hands was main way Timothy was ordained into ministry by the elders. Second Timothy 1:6 affirms that there definitely was a gift of God, an inner fire that was deposited into Timothy through the laying on of hands by the elders. This is why in many Christian circles you see

Ordination Candidates having hands laid upon them. The Anointing is transferable! The Fire of God is transferable!

Anointed for God's Assignment

Acts 13:2-3 AMP
2 While they were worshiping the Lord and fasting,
the Holy Spirit said, Separate now for Me Barnabas
and Saul for the work to which I have called them.
3 Then after fasting and praying, they put their
hands on them and sent them away.

God uses the laying on of hands to separate people for a certain work or assignment. Many times fasting and prayer are involved in the process.

Exodus 35:30-34 AMP
30 And Moses said to the Israelites, See, the Lord
called by name Bezalel son of Uri, the son of Hur, of
the tribe of Judah;
31 And He has filled him with the Spirit of God,
with ability and wisdom, with intelligence and
understanding, and with knowledge
and all craftsmanship,
32 To devise artistic designs, to work in gold,
silver, and bronze,
33 In cutting of stones for setting, and in carving of
wood, for work in every skilled craft.
34 And God has put in Bezalel's heart that he may
teach, both he and Aholiab son of Ahisamach,
of the tribe of Dan.

Even in the Old Testament God placed His Anointing upon people for special assignments. Bezalel, son of Uri was filled with the Spirit of God with ability, wisdom, intelligence, understanding, knowledge and all craftsmanship to work on God's Temple. Bezalel was anointed with the ability to devise artistic designs and much more. Did you ever think a person could be anointed to paint a picture? Have you ever seen a piece of art that brought a sense of God's Presence to you? It was an anointed piece of artwork!

I believe some people are anointed by God to work in the nursery at church. When my children were babies there was an older lady who ran the nursery. She was one of the few people I ever knew to be anointed to do the baby nursery! She told me that she prayed over each and every one of those babies. I could sense the difference she made!

God anoints people to write new songs and books! When you read an anointed book such as this book, the Anointing that God placed upon the book when it was written will transfer to the hungry reader! When you hear an anointed song, the Anointing upon the song as it was written or recorded will transfer to the hungry listener!

God anoints people to be doctors, lawyers, teachers, librarians, moms, dads, and pilots. God anoints some people to be strong in the business world. God anoints some people to finance His Kingdom. God gives people creative ideas and witty inventions and then anoints them to carry the ideas and inventions out. God anoints people to sing and play instruments. Allow God to anoint you.

Receiving the "Transference of Anointing" is not enough. We must use the Anointing God has placed upon us.

The Holy Spirit Is Received Through The Laying On Of Hands

Acts 8:17 AMP
17 Then [the apostles] laid their hands on them one by one, and they received the Holy Spirit.

Acts 19:6 AMP
*6 And as Paul laid his hands upon them, the Holy
Spirit came on them; and they spoke in [foreign,
unknown] tongues (languages) and prophesied.*

The Baptism of the Holy Spirit can be received and transferred by the laying on of hands. Laying on of hands is not
the only way for people to receive the Baptism of the Holy
Spirit with the Bible evidence of speaking in tongues. It is
one of the ways.

The Anointing Is Transferred Through
The Spoken Word

Psalms 107:20 AMP
*20 He sends forth His word and heals them and
rescues them from the pit and destruction.*

Matt 8:10,13 AMP
*8 But the centurion replied to Him, Lord, I am not
worthy or fit to have You come under my roof; but
only speak the word, and my servant
boy will be cured.*
*13 Then to the centurion Jesus said, Go; it shall be
done for you as you have believed. And the servant
boy was restored to health at that very moment.*

Just as Jesus only spoke the word for the centurion's son
to be healed, Jesus can have you speak an anointed word and
people will be healed. This is an example of words transferring the Anointing.

Words spoken, written or sung under the Anointing carry
life-changing properties! I have heard it said that words are
containers for power! Proverbs18:21 tells us that the power
of life and death are in the tongue. I cannot stress enough the

importance of receiving and operating daily in the speaking of tongues! It is a sure fire way to keep your tongue speaking properly.

Generational Transference

Ex 20:5-6 AMP
5 You shall not bow down yourself to them or serve them; for I the Lord your God am a jealous God, visiting the iniquity of the fathers upon the children to the third and fourth generation of those who hate Me, [Isaiah 42:8; 48:11.]
6 But showing mercy and steadfast love to a thousand generations of those who love Me and keep My commandments.

Some of you have probably seen the Lipitor commercial about high cholesterol. The commercial states that high cholesterol can come from what you eat or from a relative. Basically you may have inherited a bad gene pool causing you to have high cholesterol.

Many of you have heard about "generational curses". An example of a "generational curse" is out of control anger. If out of control anger runs down your family line, then you are more prone to have uncontrolled anger than someone who came from a family line that does not operate in uncontrolled anger. You have basically inherited a bad gene pool of anger.

Alcoholism and drug addiction may be a generational curse your family deals with. One drink could cause an addiction because it is a generational family curse. A person who does not have alcoholism and drug addiction in their family line more than likely will not be tempted by drugs or alcohol. One drink would not cause them to move into alcoholism. The great news is the Anointing destroys the yoke of curses! Remember when something is destroyed, it cannot be put back together again! You can be totally free from every generational curse in the Name of Jesus!

Isaiah 10:27 KJV
27 And it shall come to pass in that day, that his burden shall be taken away from off thy shoulder, and his yoke from off thy neck, and the yoke shall be destroyed because of the Anointing.

If you would like to be set free from any generational curse(s), please pray the following prayer out loud or if you prefer, have someone pray with you:

Father,
I come to you in the Name of Jesus. Your Word says that the Anointing destroys the Yoke—the burden. I ask You to remove and destroy the yoke of the generational curse(s) of_____ [you fill in the blank(s)].

Generational curse(s) of _____, I command you to leave me now in the Name of Jesus! I decree that I, who Jesus has set free, am free indeed!

I plead the Blood of Jesus over the generational curse(s) of _____. I decree that the generational curse(s) of _____, is now under the blood of Jesus and it will not ever touch me again!

I am free in the Name of Jesus! Thank you Father! Thank you Jesus! Thank you Holy Spirit!

And now, Holy Spirit I ask you to fill the empty space the generational curse took with Your Presence and power! Come and fill me Holy Spirit! I welcome you in!

In Jesus Name,
Amen

Thank Jesus for healing you. Now go and tell someone what Jesus did for you!

If you can believe in "generational curses", then why not believe in "the generational blessings" spoken about in Exodus 20:6? His blessings go to a thousand generations! I can speak from experience about generational Anointing. My mother was anointed when she sang. Two people can sing the same song. One will be anointed and the song will bring God's Presence. The other will just be another song being sung. The Anointing makes all the difference. I believe that the Anointing that is upon my singing was passed down from my mother, but I had to receive and operate in the Anointing.

God is a generational God. Someone has to receive the Anointing to begin with. Once you receive the Anointing to do something, you can see that Anointing transfer to your children. My prayer is that the Anointing that Eddie and I flow in will not only transfer to our children and children's children, but that with each generation the Anointing will grow stronger! I know from experience that I have had a greater sensitivity to the Anointing because of my parents loving God and moving in His Anointing

My dad had an Anointing to preach and win people to the Lord. My dad would lead people to the Lord on the golf course, on the job or wherever he was. My dad was a walking revival. As far back as I can remember I would invite my friends to come to church with me. When I was fourteen years old, I began inviting all of the neighbor kids to come to church with me. The church we attended had to provide us with a vehicle so we could bring them to church. Our church did not have a "bus ministry". No one encouraged me to go knocking on my neighbor's doors to invite him or her to church. Leading people to the Lord just came naturally to me. Why? I believe it was passed down from my dad and his parents.

Recently, I was speaking with my cousin, Reverend Mary Hicks. She told me that my dad was relentless in witnessing to her brothers about Jesus. Mary said she would tell her brothers to leave Teddy alone because they would pick on him. My dad had the last laugh. All of Mary's brothers with one exception received Jesus. Four of the boys became ministers of the Gospel. Mary is in the ministry with her husband of 50 years, Bill Hicks. Many children and children's children of these same cousins are now in the ministry. I believe that my children will receive an even greater Anointing than I have. There are levels of the Anointing. We go from glory to glory!

2 Corinthians 3:18 KJV
18 But we all, with open face beholding as in a
glass the glory of the Lord, are changed into the
same image from glory to glory, even as by the
Spirit of the Lord.

You say, "I have not had the privilege of coming from a godly heritage." I say, "You press into God with abandon and become the spark that gets God's fire going down your family line!" Someone has to be the beginning. You start forming the godly heritage for your family. Let the Anointing not only go down your family line, but up to your parents, aunts, uncles, and grandparents! It is time for you to transfer the Anointing!

CHAPTER TWELVE

YOU ARE NOW ENTERING THE MISSION FIELD

2 Corinthians 5:18-20 NIV
18 All this is from God, who reconciled us to
himself through Christ and gave us the ministry
of reconciliation: 19 that God was reconciling
the world to himself in Christ, not counting men's
sins against them. And he has committed to us the
message of reconciliation. 20 We are therefore
Christ's ambassadors, as though God were making
his appeal through us. We implore you on Christ's
behalf: Be reconciled to God.

Acts 1:8-9 AMP
8 But you shall receive power (ability, efficiency,
and might) when the Holy Spirit has come upon
you, and you shall be My witnesses in Jerusalem
and all Judea and Samaria and to the ends
(the very bounds) of the earth.
9 And when He had said this, even as they were
looking [at Him], He was caught up, and a cloud
received and carried Him away out of their sight.

Here is your mission should you decide to accept it. We cannot camp in the Upper Room forever. God calls you an Ambassador for Christ! You are a representative for Christ here on the earth! Every believer has been given "The Ministry of Reconciliation" according to 2 Corinthians 5:18. Some of you are saying, "I did not know that I was given a ministry by God. What is the "Ministry of Reconciliation"? The Ministry of Reconciliation is bringing people and God together. It is letting people know that because of the price that Jesus Christ paid on the cross for their sins, they can be forgiven of their sins.

We can't stay in discipleship classes forever. Not that there is anything wrong with discipleship. We must follow the original pattern given to us in the Bible. Once the 120 were filled or empowered with ability, efficiency, and might of the Holy Spirit and fire in the Upper Room, they did not camp on their experience! Their experience caused them to leave the Upper Room and take the Anointing to the streets of Jerusalem and eventually to the uttermost parts of the earth! Jerusalem represents your hometown. Judea represents the towns surrounding your hometown. Samaria represents further out than that until you get to the uttermost parts of the earth.

So many times we think the mission field is some foreign country. Although foreign countries are mission fields, so are your next-door neighbors a mission field if they don't know Jesus. So is the clerk at your local drive through window or the check out clerk at your local supermarket part of the mission field. The mission field is everyone everywhere around you. You are going to be surprised how many people have never even heard of Jesus until you tell them!

As Ecclesiastes 3:1 tells us "there is a time for everything". I add—a time to sit, soak and get anointed with the Presence and power of the Holy Spirit and a time to take what you've received and get up and go tell, heal, deliver, set free and be obedient! We are called to bind up and heal the broken hearted. Unfortunately, far too many Christians become spiritual alcoholics and just keep sitting in meeting after meeting and having another "drink" of the Holy Spirit Anointing without ever giving out. They just want to "feel good" and lay on the floor and party.

Since Acts chapter two is the birth of "The Church" and God's model for "The Church" today, then we must admit that the infilling and Anointing of the Holy Spirit is to leave the drinking and soaking party—the Upper Room experience and share the joy, Anointing, and infilling with others. The Anointing is for us to become Christ Ambassadors to a lost and dying world! When I speak of "The Church", I am speaking of the entire Body of Christ worldwide—not an individual congregation.

How Do I Allow The Anointing To Flow Through Me?

You yield! We go out and tell other people about our wonderful Lord and Savior, Jesus Christ, just like they did after being filled with the Holy Spirit in the Upper Room! When you are so saturated and filled with the Holy Spirit you cannot help but share Jesus with others! After the Holy Ghost's wild display on The Day of Pentecost, as the people left the Upper Room, about three thousand people received Jesus Christ as their Lord and Savior [Acts 2:41]. And very likely that number did not include the women and children.

Unfortunately, many think that praying for the sick is supposed to happen in the church. Many people think that almost everything is supposed to happen in the church. Not so! Not according to the book of Acts. Not according to the Bible. The Bible blueprint is to go out and bring them in, not to sit inside and wait for them to come to us!

We can pray for the sick in the market place like Peter and John did. They saw the sick healed and 5,000 people saved that same day because those 5,000 people witnessed the miracle in the streets [See Acts chapters three and four]. Most people are extremely open to someone praying for them. Praying for people can give us entrance to share Jesus with them in a non-threatening way. Again, we should use what I refer to as "Prayer Etiquette". Ask the person if they would mind if you prayed for them. Ask them if they would mind if you put your hand on them or joined hands with them. Placing your hand on a person's shoulder is usually okay. It is preferable for men to pray with men and women with women. Follow the leading of the Holy Spirit at all times. Most people are pleased that anyone cares enough to take the time to listen and pray with them.

We can allow the Holy Spirit to flow through us by obeying God's leading to go somewhere we were not planning to go. God may tell you to go to a park and sit on the bench. Then He may lead you to pray with the first person that sits down. I have heard many testimonies about people who were going to commit suicide and God placed an obedient child of His in their path at just the right moment at just the right place.

We can allow God to use us to lead someone to the Lord, baptize him or her in water, and then be translated by the Holy Spirit to another location to begin preaching the gospel like Philip did [See Acts 8:26-40].

Word of Knowledge

We can have a "Word of Knowledge" like Jesus did for the Samaritan woman at the well in John 4. The woman not only got saved, but she ran and told her entire town, "Come, see a Man Who has told me everything that I ever did! Can this be [is not this] the Christ? [Must not this be the Messiah, the Anointed one?]" Numerous Samaritans from that town believed in and trusted in Jesus because the woman at the well told them, "He told me everything that I ever did." That is how a "Word of Knowledge" catches the unbeliever. God tells you some knowledge about the person that you do not know except God told you. The person knows you could not have possibly known what God tells you to say to them.

When the Samaritans arrived at the well to meet Jesus, Jesus stayed with them for two days. Then many more believed in Jesus because of what Jesus Himself said. The people told the woman, "Now we no longer believe in Jesus as the Messiah because of what you said, but because we have heard Him for ourselves and know that He truly is the Christ, the Savior of the world" [John 4:6-42 AMP].

Jesus' obedience to give the "word of knowledge" to the Samaritan woman, not only resulted in her salvation, but many people from her town also received Jesus Christ as their Lord and Savior! Our obedience to give a person a "Word of Knowledge" that God gives us for them, can easily result in the person getting saved as well as the person's entire city receiving Jesus Christ as their Lord and Savior today!

Giving

When the Holy Spirit Anointing came upon the 120 in the upper room, every one of them became extremely effective in soul winning. Every one of them became generous and sold what they had and gave to those in need [Acts 2:44-45].

My sister, Terri Bass, shared a true story with me that her pastor shared with their congregation. God spoke to him to give $50.00 to a lady. The pastor argued with God that it was his last $50.00. God spoke to the pastor again and said, "I want you to give the lady your last $50.00." The pastor finally gave in and gave the lady the $50.00. Several months passed by and the lady came up to him and said, "Do you remember me?" He said, "Yes". The lady proceeded to tell the pastor that before he handed her the $50.00, she had prayed and asked God for some money to buy her children some Christmas presents because she did not have the money to buy them one item. She told the pastor, "If you had not given me the $50.00 that day, my children would not have had Christmas. Thank you." What if the pastor would not have been obedient? It is so critical to be obedient to God in our giving. This subject alone would take an entire book.

On several occasions, my husband and I have been in line at a store when the person in front of us did not have enough money to pay for all of their items. They needed to decide what to put back. God has directed either my husband or myself or both of us to pay for the person's things and tell them God loves them. I don't know who gets more shocked, the person receiving the blessing or the clerk behind the counter! The Anointing will cause you to become a giver! Have you ever thought about taking someone who does not know Jesus out to breakfast and then to church? Allow yourself to become sensitive to the Holy Spirit's leading.

Be Creative

Luke 5:29-32 AMP
29 And Levi (Matthew) made a great banquet
for Him in his own house, and there was a large
company of tax collectors and others who were
reclining [at the table] with them.
30 Now the Pharisees and their scribes were
grumbling against Jesus' disciples, saying, Why
are you eating and drinking with tax collectors and
[preeminently] sinful people?
31 And Jesus replied to them, It is not those who are
healthy who need a physician,
but those who are sick.

*32 I have not come to arouse and invite and call
the righteous, but the erring ones (those not free
from sin) to repentance [to change their minds for
the better and heartily to amend their ways, with
abhorrence of their past sins].*

Let our creative God give you creative ideas to reach out
to people. After all, you are His creation. Matthew, one of
the twelve disciples, got creative and made a great banquet
at his house for Jesus. Matthew basically invited a bunch of
sinners. The "religious" people complained that Jesus and
his disciples were fellowshipping with sinful people. Jesus'
reply to them was, "It is not those who are healthy who need
a physician, but those who are sick. I have not come to invite
the righteous, but those not free from sin."

Maybe you have the gift of hospitality. Invite some people
over for dinner or dessert. My daughter, Jen got the anointed
idea to have "game nights" at our home. She would invite
co-workers, acquaintances, family and friends. Everyone
that wanted to bring a snack to share was welcome to do so.
Most of those people would never dream of walking into a
church and yet through the creative idea of "game night",
several of the people received Jesus as their Savior. Some
were baptized in water and others even received the Baptism
of the Holy Spirit. People are looking for acceptance. People
are looking for God's love and do not know it. What they are
not looking for is some pious, religious, stuffed shirt, who
looks down their nose at them!

John Paul Jackson trains teams to minister through dream
interpretation and sees many souls saved. I heard Doug
Addison say we should use comedy to reach people. I've
seen puppet shows resulting in children, as well as adults
receiving Jesus. The sky is the limit! If you enjoy baking, let
God use your anointed baked goods to bring people into His

Kingdom. If you have the gift of writing anointed letters and notes, let God use your anointed writing to reach the lost!

Don't be "religious"! These people look like the world, sound like the world and smell like the world. Remember, someone needs you to be anointed! Their healing, salvation, miracle depends upon your staying filled up with the Anointing! Do not get discouraged. The Bible tells us that some plant, some water, but God gives the increase [1 Corinthians 3:7-8]. Just be obedient to do your part and leave the rest to God! I like to say it like this; "I will do what I can do in the "natural" and allow God to put His "super" on it." Now that is "supernatural"! You will find that you and God make a great team!

CHAPTER THIRTEEN

TESTIMONIES

To God Be The Glory, Great Things He Has Done!

Revelation 12:11 NIV
11 They overcame him by the blood of the Lamb
and by the word of their testimony; they did not love
their lives so much as to shrink from death.

2 Corinthians 4:15 AMP
15 For all [these] things are [taking place] for
your sake, so that the more grace (divine favor
and spiritual blessing) extends to more and more
people and multiplies through the many, the more
thanksgiving may increase [and redound]
to the glory of God.

Revelation 19:1 AMP
1 AFTER THIS I heard what sounded like a mighty
shout of a great crowd in heaven, exclaiming,
Hallelujah (praise the Lord)! Salvation and glory
(splendor and majesty) and power (dominion and
authority) [belong] to our God!

I believe that a great ending to any meal is a really great dessert! I pray that these testimonies will not only be a blessing to you, but that your faith will be stirred to receive your healing spiritually, physically, mentally, or financially. Whatever you need, God is your answer. God's Presence— God's Anointing is present right now to heal you wherever you hurt! Receive all that God has for you today!

My Personal Testimony

Back in the spring of 1984, to my utter surprise, I had a vision as I was standing in the choir loft of the church we were attending. In the vision my husband Eddie and I were standing with our hands outstretched to a group of people who I could never see the end of. On both sides of Eddie and me were other husband and wife teams doing the same thing. The sea of faces of the people we were praying for was endless. I knew by the Holy Spirit that these people were being healed spiritually, physically, mentally and financially. We were never able to lay our hands upon them. We just stood in front of the crowd and prayed for them with our hands outstretched to them. Since having a vision was so completely unusual for me at that time in my life, I told no one and forgot about it. About a month later the same thing happened. I was up in the choir loft during praise and worship and I had the same vision. God had gotten my attention! I told Eddie about it and he told me that he kept hearing God say that music was going to be a big part of the way God was going to use us. At that point we both sang in the choir and ensemble. I sang with a couple of trios. Neither of us was playing an instrument. As the Bible says, "Let God be true and every man a liar" [Romans 3:4]! Probably the most effective way God uses us today and has used us is through an Anointing for and through music and a healing Anointing.

Eddie and I were both extremely hungry for more of God than we had experienced in the past. We began devouring every book we could get on revival. We got tired just hearing about revival and yet not experiencing revival! We had pioneered our first church in March 1988 and by December of 1992 we were burnt out. Looking back, we actually had a very nice church. We had an awesome board! We had people who loved us. We had a great team of volunteers—the best we've ever had! We had a full-blown children's program! The Anointing of the Holy Spirit was present in the services. But due to our hunger for more of God, we thought we were failures and wanted to quit the ministry.

Eddie and I were lying in bed one Saturday evening in December talking about quitting the church. Eddie said, "Let's quit and go somewhere else." I said, "If it does not work here, why export it?" The phone rang and it was the daughter of our wonderful head usher, Jim Damron. Her name was Kathy. She was ordained with the Assemblies of God and had a beautiful and anointed singing voice. We would have her sing anytime she came into town to see her parents. Kathy had called to let us know that she was in town and that she felt like God had given her a word to share with the church. Eddie said, "Sure, Kathy, you can share the word God has given to you in the morning service." What Eddie did not tell Kathy is that he was thinking, "If Mickey Mouse or Donald Duck wanted to come and speak, I would let them. I don't want to preach and neither does Becky."

Sunday morning Eddie and I went through the motions of doing the praise and worship. Kathy sang a beautiful anointed song and then began to preach. All I can remember Kathy saying was "Don't quit. Don't leave, you'll be out of the ark of God's safety." At which point I looked at Eddie with that "You told her didn't you!" Eddie looked at me with "You told her didn't you!" We immediately realized that the only person who could have told Kathy besides me or Eddie was God. Then Kathy said, "Hang on your miracle is right around the corner". After comparing notes with Eddie, when Kathy said, "Hang on, your miracle is around the corner", we both had a vision of being 99 years old, holding onto a cane and rounding that corner and keeling over and dying. That is how depressed we both were. Before this time, we were always blessed that if one of us were down, the other one would be up. Unfortunately, we were both down—way down!

Here comes the altar call. Kathy said, "Does anyone need prayer?" I am sitting there thinking I do, but at that time I thought as a pastor I was not suppose to have any problems. Before I knew it, I was raising my hand and saying as I was weeping uncontrollably, "Well, I don't know if anyone else needs prayer, but I do!" I proceeded to tell everyone about our conversation in bed the previous evening, at which point Eddie decided he not only needed prayer, but also better start looking for a new job. So Eddie came down for prayer with me. The board all came and laid their hands upon Eddie and me and told us to take a week off. My dad and mom, Ted and Geneva Farina were our greatest supporters. Dad said he would preach Sunday night so we could go ahead and start our sabbatical immediately. Like I said, we really had a great group of people!

Eddie called his parents in Clinton, Maryland and asked if we could come up for a week. Eddie's parents had five beautiful acres of land with a beautiful home. Eddie had predetermined that he was going to go out on the five acres to a hill that was out there where God was going to speak to him. Eddie left on his pilgrimage. After a couple of hours out in the snow and cold he returned. I was anxiously anticipating what Eddie had heard from God. Eddie said, "I did not hear anything. I just got tired and cold." No lightning. No thunder. Nothing. Ugh!

I kept holding onto the words, "Hold on, your miracle is right around the corner". What does "right around the corner" mean to God? By February 1993, I began to get really weary of waiting for that "miracle". I had been at the church office and came home to make dinner. I turned the television on and 700 Club was on. Pat Robertson was speaking and he said, "Hold on, your miracle is right around the corner." I was ecstatic! I got dinner started and went back to the office and told Eddie all about it. They usually replayed the morning program in the evening. We sat down to watch the evening showing and to my astonishment, Pat Robertson did not say, "Hold on, your miracle is right around the corner." I decided that God let me hear what He wanted me to hear. It gave me the faith to hang on.

March 1993 we hear about a crazy South African evangelist holding a revival at Carpenters Home Church in Lakeland, Florida. Everything we heard sounded like "nuts and flakes" until one Wednesday evening. My husband was taking testimonies from people and a lady from our congregation who had attended one of the revival meetings said, "And a physically drunken man ran forward during the preaching asking how he could be saved." God spoke to Eddie and said, "Eddie, nobody is running to the front to get saved here."

That night Eddie had a dream with the headlines of the newspaper saying, "Greatest Revival in History and Dumbo Stays Home". It haunted him all day Thursday until Eddie decided that we were going to go to Lakeland that night. Our children had a day off from school on Friday, so this was a perfect opportunity to "check it out". We finished eating dinner and were getting ready to go out and get in the van when Eddie said, "I feel like a Mack truck hit me today. We are not going." So we all set our stuff down and began to go about our business. I took my shoes off and Eddie said, "Get ready, we are going to Lakeland." So I put my shoes back on. We get ready again and Eddie changes his mind again. This went on for some time until we were going to be late if we did not get on the road. It usually took about 1 hour to get to Lakeland from our home. Finally! We were all in the van headed for Lakeland. What should have taken a little more than 1 hour took us at least three hours. It was raining heavily and the traffic was horrible on Interstate 4. We had reached the Sea World exit and it was raining so heavily that Eddie said, "Let's just turn around and go back home". At that point it would have taken as long to get home, as it would have taken to get to Lakeland.

The last time we were at Carpenter's Home Church it was for a Carmen concert. There were so many people there that we had to sit in the balcony that had not been finished yet. We sat on cement and my "sitter" was not happy. I told Eddie if the only seats left were up in the balcony, I was going back home! I refused to sit on the cement again!

We remembered the revival meetings were being broadcast over the radio so we turned the program on. I could not believe my ears, "There is still room for more people, so come on out to Carpenter's Home Church where we are baptizing some 1500 people in water." Ugh! We were sitting in heavy raining traffic to go to a baptismal service where 1500 people were going to be baptized in water? I could just see it now, "In the Name of the Father, Son and Holy Spirit...1500 times! I thought, "They will be baptizing into next week!" Eddie said, "Oh, I forgot she told me they were having a water baptismal service on Thursday night."

It gets even better. We finally arrive at Carpenters Home Church and no one is at the doors to greet us. We see these people walking around in white pants with a white robe like thing on. At this point I am thinking that this is some kind of cult or something. Eddie and I are pleading the blood of Jesus over us and over our children. Since we could not find an usher to help us find a seat, I reminded Eddie that I refused to sit on the cement in the balcony. Eddie said, "Just follow me!"

The corridor where all the entry doors were located was 1/5th of a mile long. We started on one end and it was packed. By the time we reached the 3rd to the last door, four seats opened up—the people said they had to leave and offered us their seats on the back row. Exactly what we needed. Four seats! The praise and worship was still going on even though we were very late. There was a great big above ground swimming pool up in the front of the 10,000-seat auditorium. There were even more of those people dressed in white. I saw teenagers being carried out laughing. In fact, many of the things I saw I was not sure I cared for.

The praise and worship was anointed. In fact, I was really enjoying the praise and worship. Then this guy came to the platform and started singing along with the worship leader. I said to Eddie, "I don't know who that guy is. I wish he would sit down and let the praise and worship continue." It turned out to be the evangelist, Rodney Howard-Browne.

Rodney Howard-Browne gave a teaching on water baptism that was very sound. Then the water baptism began. Remember, we were not sure if the revival was of God or not, so we were listening with skeptical ears. The people in the white garb were there to help with the water baptism. Seven of them would get in the pool to baptize people. Some of them were there to help the people climb the ladder into the pool and some of them were there to help the people come down the ladder on the other side of the pool. Some of the people in white had mops to mop up some of the water. There was plastic laid all over around the pool and on the platform.

The first seven people had gone into the pool for water baptism along with the first seven people in white. The instructions to the people in white were if the people do not go out in the Spirit, then dunk them in the pool. The people who do go out in the Spirit, fish them out so they do not drown. Rodney said a general baptismal prayer and then shouted, "FILLED"! As Rodney shouted, "FILLED", it was as if a tidal wave came from the front of the auditorium and crashed on us in the back row! With each new group, Rodney would yell, "FIRE" or something like it. Each time the wave of the Anointing would come crashing upon us in the back row. There is one thing Eddie and I know. We know God and this was God! We may not have liked everything we saw, but we knew God was there big time! We sat there until after midnight watching people be baptized and getting hit with the Anointing! It seemed like minutes. We ended up taking our children out of school for some of the revival meetings because we knew it was historical in nature. They both still received straight A's that semester! Do not underestimate what God can do!

It would take an entire book to record what happened to Eddie and me at those revivals in 1993. We were believers! I am going to share one of the greatest experiences we had which took place on April 1, 1993. The significance of the date is that my husband proposed to me on April 1, 1977. He was very romantic about it. He borrowed his dad's black Cadillac and drove me out to the beach. Since Eddie loves to play April Fools jokes, I thought the proposal was a very bad April Fools joke and threw the ring back at him. After seeing the look on his face, I realized that this was a real proposal and the rest is history.

Rodney had told all the pastors to be at the April 1st morning meeting because he was going to transfer the Anointing to the pastors. We believe in the transference of Anointing. The service was coming to an end and Rodney asked for the Pastors to come up first. There were about 5,000 people there that morning. We were shocked because we were actually one of the first 50 to be prayed for! I cannot tell you how many times we stood in line for over an hour to have the evangelist lay hands on us and say something like "fire". Then we would lie on the floor for another hour. We were addicted to the Presence and Anointing of God!

Eddie and I were waiting in line. We were holding hands. I don't even remember what Rodney said as he laid hands on us that day. I just knew that he was transferring the Anointing to us and I was ready to receive all that God had for me. We were both down on the floor for what seemed to be minutes. After comparing notes with each other, Eddie and I both had a sense that they left the camera lights on. Even though our eyes were closed, you could sense an extremely bright light. We also could hear someone laughing in the distance off and on. The fire of God hit both of us.

Ex 40:34 AMP
34 Then the cloud [the Shekinah, God's visible presence] covered the Tent of Meeting, and the glory of the Lord filled the tabernacle!

When we got up off the floor, it had been 3 ½ hours. Not only were the camera lights not on, the auditorium was dark. We were the only ones left in the building. How do I know that? The janitor was the one we heard off and on laughing in the distance. He said he had to stay to tell us what he saw. He said the Shekinah Glory Cloud was hovering over the two of us as we lay on the floor. That explained the sense of an extremely bright light. Eddie burned somewhere on his torso for six months. After a couple of weeks of the burning, Eddie asked God what was going on. God answered and said, "What have you been asking Me for, for the past two years?" Eddie replied, "The Holy Ghost and fire." [Luke 3:16] That's exactly what he received.

We have never been the same since. Our church went into full swing revival! When we would minister outside of our church, we purposely would not tell the people about any of the manifestations we had been seeing and were seeing as we ministered. Without fail, the same manifestations we had experienced would manifest in the services. People were being carried out drunk. People were laughing uncontrollably. Healings were taking place spiritually, physically, mentally and financially, just as God had said they would. They still are! We have seen many miracles over the years! I am only going to share a couple of the written testimonies people handed us over the years. Jesus is the same yesterday, today and forever [Hebrews 13:8]! Jesus is the healer! To God Be The Glory, Great Things He Has Done!

Healed from Epilepsy
Shirley Pyles—Camp Springs, Maryland

As a child I had spells, but was never diagnosed until I was in my twenties as being epileptic with grand mal seizures. I had to take a lot of medication every day to try to keep my seizures under control. First thing every morning when I got out of bed I would have to take my medication and wait for it to take effect before I could do anything. In June of 1993 Eddie and Becky Cain held a revival at the church I attend, Evangel Assembly of God in Camp Springs, Maryland. I went forward for prayer and I was slain in the Spirit. I knew God had healed me. After that I went to my neurologist and told him I wanted to come off all my medication, that God had healed me. After he weaned me off my medication, he sent me for an EEG. It was the first time I had a normal EEG. Praise God, I haven't had another seizure since. I thank God for my healing!

Pre-Uterine Condition Healed
Melissa Paisley—Yulee, Florida

During the first week of December 1994, I had a doctor's appointment. At that appointment the doctor said I had had an abnormal pap smear and that the cells if not taken care of could turn into cancer. I was given a prescription and in April of 1995 returned for another exam hoping it was gone. The doctor told me that it wasn't better, but getting worse. He gave me another prescription (a stronger one) and told me to return in the second week of September. I didn't because I knew it wasn't better and I didn't want to hear the news. I had really bad stomach pains on October 4th and went to the Revival on October 5th. I asked for prayer for healing and was slain in the Spirit. On October 6th (the next day) I went for another doctors appointment. The doctor said that everything was fine and there was no sign of the previous cancer! PRAISE GOD, I AM HEALED!!!

Healed of Fibromalygia and Filled with the Holy Spirit
Diane Kogok—Clinton, Maryland

Dear Becky and Eddie, I don't know if you remember me, but on March 22, 1996 you were at Clinton Christian Assembly in Clinton, Maryland. Becky's Sermon was on healing that night. I was the one with a pillow to sit on and I could hardly walk up front to get prayed for. I had been very sick since Feb. 25th, longer than that really, since Thanksgiving of 95. I had chronic pain from Fibromalygia and a bladder condition, which involves the bladder wall. There are no cures for either of these problems and doctors rarely want to treat them. God healed me on March 22. I have continued to improve everyday. I am no longer bedridden. I returned to work on May

8th. I believe that God wants to heal us. I don't think I really believed that before that night. I was blessed with the Holy Spirit and continue to speak in tongues. My muscle pain is 95% better. I know it will be 100% one day soon. I have had chronic pain of some sort since 1988. The Lord heals, but we have to receive His love or healing. That is the beauty of the Lord. We don't have to be worthy. We just need to Love Him and trust Him to receive healing of any kind. Thanks for stopping in Maryland.

Received Speaking In Tongues
Salome Broderick—Maryland

I want to share how I received the gift of speaking in tongues. The first time was at my house during my prayer time. It came so natural. Two days later during a Revival service, Evangelist Eddie Cain called people to come forward for prayer. It was during this time while I was waiting for Eddie and Becky to pray for me that I was overcome by the power of the Holy Spirit and went down and I even speak in tongues once again, but to my amazement I found that I could not speak in English or in my native tongue of Spanish for an hour and a half. My husband was concerned when he saw me because I was trying to talk, but the only words that would come out was the divine language from the Holy Spirit. This experience has richly blessed my husband and me to continue to seek His Kingdom.

Chemical Depression Healed
Sylvia Muller—Winter Springs, Florida

All my life I had been depressed, even in child-hood. Over twenty years ago, I had individual and group therapy. For many years I have been on antidepressants. The psychiatrist said I would be on them for the rest of my life because of a chemical imbalance. Jesus Christ healed me completely on January 28 & 29 1996 during three Revival services of Eddie and Becky Cain Ministries. I tapered off all anti-depressant medications. I am set free and happy. February 15, 1996, Jesus said to me, "no psychiatrist is going to get the glory for healing me because only Jesus can heal the broken hearted and set the captive free". (Isaiah 61:1)

Food Allergies Healed
Kamari Hill—Pierson, Florida
Kamari was healed of tomato allergies at the Revival meeting Sunday night 7/13/2008. Pastor Becky Cain gave a testimony of a recent healing of food allergies in her own life, and felt the Lord wanted to heal those with food allergies in the service. Pastor Becky laid hands on Kamari. The next day she ate some tomato and had no reaction after being prayed for. Thank you so much for your obedience to the Spirit.

> We love you!
> Kairon and Latoya Hill—Peirson Florida
> (Kamari's parents)

Fibromyalgia Healed
Shilretha Dixon—Deland, Florida
Several months ago, while attending during the 45 Days of Prayer for Volusia County, under the outpouring of the Holy Spirit, I was healed from fibromyalgia. Pastor Becky Cain gave a "Word of Knowledge" that I had been suffering from fibromyalgia and God wanted to heal me. She then walked over to me, asked me to lift my hands toward heaven,

after which she laid hands on me. The Glory of God was released and since that day I walk in victory healed from fibromyalgia.

Miracle Pregnancy
Theresa — Deltona, Florida

My husband and I have tried to conceive a child for seven years. I took hormones that gave me unbearable mood swings. I had undergone three abdominal surgeries in six years. I had two unsuccessful attempts at artificial insemination. I was so desperate that I even went as far as to caress Fertility Statues. We had even heard over a local radio station that a couple had the wife take some cough syrup (believed to clear up congestion) and stand on her head while they inserted his sperm with a turkey baster. As you can see we tried everything in our means that we could afford, to bear a child. I prayed, I cried, we fought. It was pure hell. We gave up for awhile. The devil lied to me. He made me believe it was best to have a total hysterectomy because of the endometriosis (an autoimmune disease) and the pain that I suffered from it, coupled with my infertility, and that was my plan.

Doctor Jesus touched me twice in 1998. In May, I was cured from endometriosis by the laying on of hands in my home by one of the church members. In June my pastor laid hands on my belly and she announced, "Baby come forth". I was slain in the Spirit and felt a slight tingling in my belly. When the service was over and as I was driving home, I explained to the passengers in my car that something happened to my belly today. All I knew is it would never be the same. We had a Camp Meeting in August. One night I went forward for prayer. I was praising

God, and thanking him for the baby he would send me. I was crying and laughing, the Anointing was very strong. I also promised him that because of this I would give him all the Glory. I came home that night, and told my husband that we had to go make a baby, because the Anointing of the Lord was upon me. He thought I was crazy! That is when the second miracle took place. I became pregnant for the first time in my life at the age of thirty-five.

I am also not proud to say that I have had two sexually transmitted diseases. That alone, will cause you to be sterile. You see my point is that the devil gave me his best shots. My God is so awesome, and so much bigger than the devil is.

I will close in saying that God loves you, and He has a plan for your life. If you have lost hope, come to the cross where the healing river flows!

Jesus Is The Same Yesterday, Today and Forever

Since Jesus is the same yesterday, today and forever, then it is time for you to receive your healing right now! Read the healing scriptures below.

Isaiah 53:4-5 AMP
4 Surely He has borne our griefs (sicknesses,
weaknesses, and distresses) and carried our
sorrows and pains [of punishment],
yet we [ignorantly] considered Him stricken,
smitten, and afflicted by God
[as if with leprosy]. [Matt 8:17.]
5 But He was wounded for our transgressions,
He was bruised for our guilt and iniquities; the
chastisement [needful to obtain]
peace and well-being for us was upon Him,

and with the stripes [that wounded] Him we are
healed and made whole.

1 Peter 2:24 AMP
24 He personally bore our sins in His [own] body
on the tree [as on an altar and offered Himself on
it], that we might die (cease to exist) to sin and live
to righteousness. By His wounds
you have been healed.

Matthew 8:2-3 AMP
2 And behold, a leper came up to Him and,
prostrating himself, worshiped Him, saying, Lord,
if You are willing, You are able to
cleanse me by curing me.
3 And He reached out His hand and touched him,
saying, I am willing; be cleansed by being cured.
And instantly his leprosy was cured and cleansed.

In Matthew 8:3, Jesus tells the leper that He is not only able, but He is willing to cure the man's leprosy. Jesus is telling you right now, "I Am willing to heal you!" Many people believe that God "can" heal them. The disconnect comes in believing God is "willing" to heal them. If God is not willing to heal all, then you and I would determine that we are surely the exception and it is not God's will to heal us. It is God's will to heal you right now! We will not need to experience healing in heaven since there is no sickness in heaven [Revelation 21:4]!

Unfortunately, many pulpits proclaim the need to pray for the sick with the statement, "If it be Your will." IT IS GOD'S WILL TO HEAL each and every one of us! Otherwise, Jesus is a schizophrenic. Jesus was tortured and died on the cross that by His torture—the stripes that wounded Him, and by His dying on the cross we would be healed and made whole!

Therefore, it is God's will for you to be healed right now! Jesus already paid for your healing with His life! Your part is to believe and receive His healing. He has already provided everything you need! When receiving their healing, some people feel a heat come on the part of their body that has the sickness. Some people feel chill bumps. Some feel nothing. If you need healing, spiritually, physically, mentally, or financially, pray this prayer out loud and receive your God-given healing right now!

Heavenly Father,

I come to you In The Name of Jesus. Your Word says that by Jesus Christ's stripes I was and I am healed. I believe that Jesus died on the cross for my sins and for my sicknesses: spiritually, physically, mentally and financially! I receive my healing right now by faith. [List the healings you are receiving at this time.] Thank You for healing me! Thank You for the price that was paid for my healing! Thank You for the cross Lord! I decree that I am the healed of the Lord! God's healing power is working through me right now! I decree that this sickness will not return a second time [Nahum 1:9]!

In the Name of Jesus,
Amen

Now, continue to thank Jesus for your healing. The next step is to share your testimony with others. Tell someone what God has done for you.

When you see or hear about a need for healing spiritually, physically, mentally, or financially, offer to pray with them and let God's healing Anointing flow through you to touch and change your world!

Mark 16:15-20 AMP
15 And He said to them, Go into all the world and
preach and publish openly the good news (the
Gospel) to every creature
[of the whole human race].
16 He who believes [who adheres to and trusts in
and relies on the Gospel and Him Whom it sets
forth] and is baptized will be saved [from the
penalty of eternal death]; but he who does not
believe [who does not adhere to and trust in and
rely on the Gospel and Him Whom it sets forth]
will be condemned.
17 And these attesting signs will accompany those
who believe: in My name they will dr
18 They will pick up serpents; and [even] if they
drink anything deadly, it will not hurt them; they
will lay their hands on the sick,
and they will get well.
19 So then the Lord Jesus, after He had spoken to
them, was taken up into heaven and He sat down at
the right hand of God. [Ps 110:1.]
20 And they went out and preached everywhere,
while the Lord kept working with them and
confirming the message by the attesting signs and
miracles that closely accompanied [it].
Amen (so be it).

CONCLUSION

2 Corinthians 4:7 KJV
7 But we have this treasure in earthen vessels, that
the excellency of the power may be of God,
and not of us.

The Bibles tells us that we have this treasure—The Anointing, God's manifested Presence—in frail human bodies. He is the treasure! Treasure chests are usually locked and they require a "key" to open the lock. A treasure brings to mind, gold, jewels and wealth. God has deposited into all of us something of far greater value, the treasure of His Presence and all that His Presence entails! The Bible tells us that in His Presence is fullness of joy!

Ps 16:11 AMP
11 You will show me the path of life; in Your
presence is fullness of joy, at Your right hand there
are pleasures forevermore. [Acts 2:25-28,31.]

God has given us 7 Keys to unlock the Anointing—God's manifested, tangible, Presence in our lives. We must choose to take the 7 Keys and unlock the Anointing that not only resides in us, but is also waiting to be unleashed through us to touch and change the world.

In the second half of 2 Corinthians 4:7, God specifies why He has chosen to put the Anointing in earthen vessels like you and me. To show the world that His manifested, tangible Presence in our lives is from Him and not from us! To make sure that God gets all the glory due Him. First Corinthians 10:31 tells us that whether we eat or drink, or whatever we do, do it all for the honor and glory of God.

Matthew 22:37-40 AMP
37 And He replied to him, You shall love the Lord
your God with all your heart and with all your soul
and with all your mind (intellect).
38 This is the great (most important, principal)
and first commandment.
39 And a second is like it: You shall love your
neighbor as [you do] yourself.
40 These two commandments sum up and upon
them depend all the Law and the Prophets

The only way the "7 Keys To The Anointing" will work for you is for you to begin using each of the 7 Keys to unlock and unleash the potential God has placed inside of you. First and foremost, is "Key #1—God's Love, The Foundational Key"! We must love God with ALL our heart, soul, mind and strength! Then we must love our neighbor as ourselves. Without the foundational key of love, the other keys will not work properly! God's love will determine what our hearts' motive is for wanting to move in God's Anointing—His manifested Presence? God is Love and without the love of God as our foundation, we are nothing more than the noisy gong or clanging cymbal First Corinthians 13:1 speaks of.

I challenge each and every one of you to implement the "7 Keys To The Anointing"! Dive into God's Presence! You will never be the same again! There are stages in allowing the Anointing or God's manifested Presence to manifest through you. With Love as your foundation, you must allow the Anointing to touch you first. Secondly, you must allow the Anointing to change you. Lastly, you must allow the Anointing to flow through you to touch and change the world! It is the gift that keeps on giving. The world is waiting for you to flow in the Anointing! Your best days are ahead!

ENDNOTES

Chapter One

[1]Nelson's Illustrated Bible Dictionary, Copyright (c)1986, Thomas Nelson Publishers

Chapter Two

[1] The New Unger's Bible Dictionary. Originally published by Moody Press of Chicago, Illinois. Copyright © 1988.

Chapter Three

[1]Biblesoft's New Exhaustive Strong's Numbers and Concordance with Expanded Greek-Hebrew Dictionary. Copyright © 1994, 2003 Biblesoft, Inc. and International Bible Translators, Inc. OT:4886

[2]Biblesoft's New Exhaustive Strong's Numbers and Concordance with Expanded Greek-Hebrew Dictionary. Copyright © 1994, 2003 Biblesoft, Inc. and International Bible Translators, Inc. NT:5548

[3]The New Unger's Bible Dictionary. Originally published by Moody Press of Chicago, Illinois. Copyright (c) 1988.

[4]Biblesoft's New Exhaustive Strong's Numbers and Concordance with Expanded Greek-Hebrew Dictionary. Copyright © 1994, 2003 Biblesoft, Inc. and International Bible Translators, Inc. NT:5545

[5]Biblesoft's New Exhaustive Strong's Numbers and Concordance with Expanded Greek-Hebrew Dictionary. Copyright © 1994, 2003 Biblesoft, Inc. and International Bible Translators, Inc. NT::1636

[6]Biblesoft's New Exhaustive Strong's Numbers and Concordance with Expanded Greek-Hebrew Dictionary. Copyright © 1994, 2003 Biblesoft, Inc. and International Bible Translators, Inc. NT::4982

[7]Biblesoft's New Exhaustive Strong's Numbers and Concordance with Expanded Greek-Hebrew Dictionary. Copyright © 1994, 2003 Biblesoft, Inc. and International Bible Translators, Inc. NT::5548

[8]Biblesoft's New Exhaustive Strong's Numbers and Concordance with Expanded Greek-Hebrew Dictionary. Copyright © 1994, 2003 Biblesoft, Inc. and International Bible Translators, Inc. NT::20

[9]Biblesoft's New Exhaustive Strong's Numbers and Concordance with Expanded Greek-Hebrew Dictionary. Copyright © 1994, 2003 Biblesoft, Inc. and International Bible Translators, Inc. OT::4643

Chapter Seven

[1]Biblesoft's New Exhaustive Strong's Numbers and Concordance with Expanded Greek-Hebrew Dictionary.

Copyright © 1994, 2003 Biblesoft, Inc. and International Bible Translators, Inc. NT:3466

Chapter Ten

[1]Biblesoft's New Exhaustive Strong's Numbers and Concordance with Expanded Greek-Hebrew Dictionary. Copyright © 1994, 2003 Biblesoft, Inc. and International Bible Translators, Inc. NT::6960

[2]Biblesoft's New Exhaustive Strong's Numbers and Concordance with Expanded Greek-Hebrew Dictionary. Copyright © 1994, 2003 Biblesoft, Inc. and International Bible Translators, Inc. NT::6960

[3]Biblesoft's New Exhaustive Strong's Numbers and Concordance with Expanded Greek-Hebrew Dictionary. Copyright © 1994, 2003 Biblesoft, Inc. and International Bible Translators, Inc. NT::6960

Chapter Eleven

[1]Nelson's Illustrated Bible Dictionary, Copyright (c)1986, Thomas Nelson Publishers

ABOUT THE AUTHOR

Reverend Becky Farina Cain has been in the full time ministry since 1988 along with her husband of 32 years, Eddie Cain. They often humorously share with their audiences that they have been Co-Pastors, Co-Praise and Worship Leaders and Co-Evangelists, so you might as well call them the "Co-Cain's".

Becky, along with her songwriter husband, has recorded several anointed Praise and Worship CD's. Becky and Eddie have ministered nationally as well as internationally.

In the spring of 1984, God visited Becky with a vision. Becky saw herself, along with her husband standing on an extremely large platform. There were husband and wife teams on both sides of Becky and Eddie. All of the couples had their hands outstretched in prayer to an endless crowd of people. In the vision Becky tried to see where the crowd ended, but it was an endless sea of faces. She could not physically touch the people because there were too many of them. Becky knew by the Holy Spirit, that the people were being healed spiritually, physically, mentally and financially. During that same time, God spoke to Eddie saying that music was going to be a big part of the way God was going to use him and Becky. The most effective way God uses Becky and Eddie today is through a healing Anointing that not only manifests when they preach/teach, but also strongly manifest through their music.

Becky and Eddie live in Florida. Both of their children are married and they have one grandson. Their daughter, Jen and son-in-law, Trey are expecting a baby. Their son Eric and daughter-in-law, Liz have a son named Peyton.

To Contact
Becky Farina Cain

Or to:
Book a Meeting
Book a three-day "In His Presence Seminar"
To purchase Anointed Praise and Worship Music

Visit our website at:
www.BeckyFarinaCain.com

LaVergne, TN USA
26 February 2010
174427LV00001B/8/P